# Water Breaking Faith
## The Aftermath of Hurricane Harvey's Path

### Lady Mary Hatter

Copyright ©2018, Lady Mary Hatter

ALL RIGHTS RESERVED.

No part of this publication may be reproduced, stored in a retrieval system, or transmitted in any form or by any means—electronic, mechanical, photo-copy, recording, or any other—except for brief quotation in reviews, without the prior permission of the author or publisher.

ISBN: 978-1-948638-77-7

Published by

Fideli Publishing, Inc.
119 W. Morgan St.
Martinsville, IN 46151

www.FideliPublishing.com

# Dedication and Acknowledgment

To my husband, Pastor A.D. Hatter, my two children, Tangeneva and Tristian. My granddaughter, Maranda, and grandson, Josiah, both from Tangeneva. I love and appreciate you all dearly.

I also dedicate this book to those of you who experienced a devastating lost, and to those that didn't. To those people who prayed for us and helped in our times of need. To all who read, I speak blessings to you indeed. Thanks to everyone who continues to sow seeds.

# Contents

*Introduction* ........................................................... vii

The Journey Begins ............................................. 1
Water Breaking Faith! ......................................... 25
Jesus is My Everything! ....................................... 61
The Campgound with Holy Ghost Fire! ............ 69
Prophecy of Prosperity ....................................... 81
Resurrection Sunday! .......................................... 87
Prayer of Thanksgiving for all that God has Given! ..... 99
No Lid ................................................................. 109
Our Set Place ..................................................... 115
Listen in! ............................................................. 121
God told me I was His MC ............................... 131
The Great Commission ..................................... 141
Conclusion ......................................................... 147

# Introduction

Praise God! I'm so overwhelmed with joy; even though the enemy sent a decoy. God's people are being led and fed by His Spirit, therefore the devil can't destroy.

As we continue to walk in willingness and obedience, we continue to eat the good of the land. We can never be destroyed by the pestilence and predators in these perilous times of the present, and the things that's coming. Know that victory has already been won, because of God's precious son!

**We experienced the tragedy of Hurricane Harvey on August 28, 2017**

We lost what we thought was everything, however He spared our lives. Thank you Lord! In this Hurricane our two-story home was flooded up to about the fourth stair heading to the second floor. Many things were lost, but to God be the glory, my family and I were rescued in boats from the very high floodwaters.

We were misplaced, but God allowed us to get in the race, as we kept up the pace. These unpleasant times, we knew we had to face. This was hard at first, but with God's Grace, I'm believing, receiving, and thanking Him for the manifestations; and I'm expecting great things to keep coming!

During our process of losing what I said was everything, my sister Juanita, while consoling me, spoke these words, "This is only a testimony for your new book."

I said, "I receive, even though this bad thing had happened to me." At the time she said this to me, I had no new book in mind yet. I was emotional, crying, and hurt, because of losing everything. I was not just out of my home; I was out of my prayer zone.

This situation and position, put me in a place where I prayed, praised, and worshiped God; and received from Him like never before. I knew I had to reposition myself for the mission and message that God would use me for. I was His Messenger.

This book came about because of what I experienced during Hurricane Harvey. God showed me that things will happen that we can't control. We must trust Him, and do what we are told, before and after things unfold. It is in Christ Jesus we behold.

We will experience things in life that are not pleasant. People, we must know that we aren't alone, even though there are times when it seems as if we are. God has allowed His Grace and the gifts to come about so that we can help others handle the different situations we experience in life.

God has sent me, His Messenger, with His message, by way of His Spirit. In this book I will share my experiences during and after Hurricane Harvey. There will be things said that I hope will show you how to deal with situations that you can't control, and things that you can control. Listen in, as I show you how to win!

This is what had to happen, because God allowed it. Let's be clear, God doesn't just make bad things happen to you; however He will allow things to come. His will has already been done. Victory, you have received because of His son.

We had to stay focused and in faith, for all the things God kept allowing to come our way in this Water Breaking Faith! The water has to break before the baby comes, then comes the blessings of God's will being done. The water was released and we were rescued from our home, even though we had no control over Hurricane Harvey, we knew that God allows us to have control of our today, and tomorrow.

I decided to partner with Holy Spirit and he guided me through my journey. I followed God's plans, because I understood this is how He blesses man and woman. These instructions were key, as He placed them in our hands.

Come walk with me and see, how we received the increase. We were pushed out of our comfort zones, and now we've come into our own. What we lost wasn't greater than what we gained, all because we kept doing things in Jesus' name. Our lives will never be the same, after experiencing this great change.

Our God is an awesome God! We shall continue to obey Him, even as we did from the start. In Christ Jesus we will not depart. We love God with all our hearts. I say thank you God for the good as well as the bad. I've chosen to rejoice and be exceedingly glad!

# The Journey Begins

As I began to write this book, it made me realize the things I wasn't aware of before the Hurricane. I came to the realization that God was preparing me, by speaking to me beforehand, that something was about to happen and what the outcome would be.

This might sound strange, however God had spoken to me in advance about how I would receive this new position in life, all because of how I had sacrificed, but kept serving. I had gone through testing times in my marriage, but I came through without the smell of smoke. Praise God! He spoke to me about how I have already received the most, as I continue to stay on my **POST**.

<u>P</u>rosperity<br>
<u>O</u>ver<br>
<u>S</u>truggling<br>
<u>T</u>imes

**New Position in Life**

   **This is what God spoke to me on July 29, 2017**: I've been reassigned, realigned, and repositioned in this Great Commission. When I speak, souls will be saved immediately because the Spirit of the Lord is upon me. I will speak to the nations, as God has blessed my generation.

I'm a God-made miracle millionaire. I'm there now. I don't know how. All this money just keeps coming about. I shout. God has brought me out. Hallelujah! Hallelujah!

People are healed, delivered, and set free from the chains that were holding them down. When I lift my hands, people dance. I receive God's plans of prosperity. I'm supernaturally debt free. I teach, I preach, I reach, and I receive my healing.

I receive my harvest, and I receive my wealth and riches that are already in my house now. I receive supernatural monies in my bank account now. I receive all my teaching engagements now. I receive all my monies from my books and UPE Designs now. My household is blessed, and the kingdom of God is blessed.

I have rest. I receive now, my new house I've been speaking out. I won't settle for less because God has given me His best. KMC has more than one location. I receive now. People are placing money in our hands. KMC is debt free.

Unconditional love is given from us and to us. We are God's beloved ones. We can never be in lack. We won't turn back. We have more than enough.

People recognize and respect our anointing. Holy Spirit keeps people that God didn't put there out of our personal space. The hedge of protection surrounds us. The blood blocks all forces of the enemy. It shall not come near us.

Wherever we dwell, that's where the Angels deliver our mail. With God we never fail. Holy Spirit is always with us, leading and guiding. Where God is, that's where we abide. The enemy can't ride or survive, because under the shadow of His almighty wings we hide.

In Him, I live, I move, I breathe, and I have my total being. God keeps blessing me season after season. I'm blessed for this very reason. The kingdom of God is at hand. He has chosen to use man and woman. I pray, I stay, and I obey what He says.

God has searched my heart, and He's set me apart. He's never far, and He will never depart. I've been blessed from the start. Dominion is my birthright. I will never lose sight. I receive, I receive, I receive, and I receive all these blessings of prosperity.

**Smell of Money**

Today there was a sweet smelling scent, and there was no one near me wearing perfume. Afterwards, God began to speak to me.

**This is what God spoke to me on August 3, 2017**: Sweet smelling savor, God has given me favor. Favor has found me. Money has found me. Money with a find. Money that makes me shine. Money that makes me look good, as I should, while walking in God's divine. I'm always on His mind. Money that keeps on looking for me. Money that's attached, attracted, and attacking me.

Everywhere I look, money is all around. Money is in my house. Money is in my bank account. More money than I can handle. Money that's tuned into my channel. Money that has made me rich and wealthy. Manifested, multiplied money. Exceedingly abundantly, above all I could have asked for money.

I'm a God-made miracle millionaire. He has allowed me to go there. He has been there before time. Even before time began. There is the place of no sins. There is where I always win. There is where God says come in. There is His place of rest, revelations, resources, reigning, remaining, revenue, reaching, and receiving all things He's restored, rendered, and released to me.

I receive all this money that God has given me. I thank God for it all. I keep standing tall. God has allowed the wall to fall. I thank Him and I continue to shout. I always remember that He allows it all to keep coming about. I'm out and He's in. I'm out of debt, and all my needs are met. God says, "You haven't seen nothing yet. My money has broken the net."

Manifested, multiplied money, supernaturally supplied, and never running out money. Unlimited money. Kingdom-building money. Money that doesn't make you sin. Boat loads of money, and bountiful living.

Believers are living and loving this life of blessings and giving. Obedience, and seed-sowing is key, for money to keep coming to me. I'm receiving and thanking God continually.

**Later this day He spoke to me again, this is what He said:**
Pay close attention to the scent and sweet smell that's satisfying to your soul. Keep sowing the seeds that the almighty God will keep giving you. Your senses have switched systems, and connected to the right surroundings. You are saturated in the Spirit, while hearing the sudden sound.

You function in the supernatural, superb situations that allow you to be solid, secure, and stationed in His Sanctuary, where souls come to hear, listen, and do, all that has been commanded. This shall keep being communicated to you.

People shall continue to get saved, and live in sanctification from the Savior. We shall keep speaking what God has said, what He's saying now, and what He will continue to speak to us about. He will keep showing us how.

Always be Spirit led, and know that He will allow you to keep being fed. Keep the sweet smell of the scent coming as you worship and praise Him. Obey, pray, stay, and listen to the Spirit. Never leave His presence. Always receive, and thank Him for it.

**God spoke to me a few days before the Hurricane.** I know now that He was preparing me for what was coming, and telling me what the result would be. He knows all, and He prepares His children before the fall, and allows them to recover all.

You shall receive the expected end, because of His plans; it's all in your hands. Stand strong, it won't be long. Quickly, suddenly, you will see! This scripture God shared with me.

> For I know the plans I have for you," says the Lord. "They are plans for good and not for disaster, to give you a future and a hope. In those days when you pray, I will listen. If you look for me wholeheartedly, you will find me. I will be found by you," says the Lord. "I will end your captivity and restore your fortunes. I will gather you out of the nations where I sent you and will bring you home again to your own land.
>
> **Jeremiah 29:11-14 NLT**

**Two days before the hurricane, August 24, 2017**: When I closed my eyes while praying in the spirit I saw this: A big city at night, with beautiful different colored lights. I saw an Angel playing a harp, also.

Even in our darkest nights, God allows our light to shine bright. It's beautiful for all the world to see. We are the show for the world to know, where He has chosen for us to go. Continue to go yea therefore with compassion, calling, and compelling people to receive our Almighty God, the one who's blessing every man and woman.

He has given us all His promises, by grace, through faith. There's a sweet sound played on a musical instrument that has strings stretched across a large open frame and it's played with our fingers. God uses this particular instrument for example, because of its large frame, to show you how far you can stretch across this world when being obedient to His will. He uses the Angel, the one who obeys our voice, and brings all things our way. When we pray, we need to always be ready to receive what God has to say.

> Know that God causes everything to work together for the good of those who love Him, and are called according to his purpose for them.
>
> **Romans 8:28 NLT**

Pay attention to the small flashes that come across your eyes, because they are blessings that can't be disguised. These are small, focus flashes that God has made to be large films, developed just for His obedient servants.

Remember the word God spoke before, about Picture in a Picture? That's what we are. We are framed, as we remain in His presence. We are flowing and flourishing films, developed by God Himself. He alone has brought us into His own: we now own this world and all that's in it.

Some things are in our control and some things are not. We control the picture; it's what we allow to be seen. However, God controls the development, which comes from our obedience, and what we allow Him to do in and through us.

**Picture in a Picture**

<u>Revelation on the Developed Pictures in a Picture:</u>

God's People Films are Developed
Great Pictures Frames are on Display
Given Plenty of Finances and Dominion

Inside the large screen, you are a High-Def Picture. In Christ Jesus, you are qualified with quality. You have been set in this large place. You are God's very best. You can't remain a small picture in a picture; you are made to be and receive large.

Tap on the big screen and the small one goes away. Without High-Def, the picture looks gray. Connect to the best, because as His children you are better than the rest.

You are God's people and your films are developed. You are great pictures set in frames displaying what He wants to be seen. No dust or rust. You've been given plenty of finances and dominion.

Look inside and see what God sees. See the big picture, not the small. There is enough prosperity for us all. Accept the call. Never fall. Don't drop the ball; you have it in your hands. Receive the plans. Make the play. Pray. Stay. Obey.

All these Blessings have come to you today. Never go astray, or lose your way. The lost have been found, and no sin can abound. God is always around. Keep standing on His Holy ground.

**August 25, 2017**

>**HI FANS**
>**H**eavens
>**I**ncrease
>
>**F**inancial
>**A**bundance and
>**N**o
>**S**hortage

You have **Heavens Increase, Financial Abundance and No Shortage.** Stay faithful, and focused on what I say to do. I've given it **ALL** to you — **A**nointing, **L**eaping and **L**ife. You grow in Leaps, and always abound. In My Word, you keep doing what you have heard. I speak even when you sleep. Yes, you heard it from Me. I Am that I Am, your almighty God of all. Stand tall.

Don't look at what people are doing or have done to you. I shall reveal, and remove all these things people think they are hiding from you. I shall expose. I shall encourage, keep the faith. You are great. Expect the great. You shall do greater.

Fly high. Supernaturally multiply. No lack. No limits. Love and love life. Keep lifting. You are gifted. I say what I say; you have been given all My promises today.

Keep reaching for what seems to be the unreachable. I shall continue to show you all things to come. Victory, victory, victory, you have won, because of My son. Jesus didn't die in vain, he gave his life for you to reign, and remain.

Your sins have been forgiven. Just keep on living. Live long, and live strong. In Christ Jesus you belong. This is a message of encouragement. Keep praying in the Spirit.

I make known what was once a mystery. Revelation knowledge, know that your sins have already been abolished. Because of the Cross of Christ, you've won the fight. Everything that was against you has been removed. Rest in Me, as I rule in you. I've made all this happen for you.

Keep praying, obeying, and staying. I have plenty to say to you. I shall keep speaking. Pay attention. My Word you must always mention, and minister to those I prepare to hear from you by way of Holy Spirit, whom I allow to speak through you.

By My Spirit, you shall keep being led, and fed. My Spirit overrules all other spirits that try to step in. In Christ Jesus you always win. Speak what you want to come your way. I shall do for you the very things I have heard you say.

Now tell them this:

> "As surely as I live, declares the Lord, I will do to you the very things I heard you say."
>
> **Numbers 14:28 NLT**

**God reminded me of what He spoke on March 7, 2017**
He said always remember these three:

1) I am not a man.

2) I can't lie.

3) I have caused things in your life to multiply.

Always have expectation and desire, and make sure your desires line up with what I've promised. You are never in need. You always have a seed. Receive. Receive. I have blessed you indeed.

I keep repeating this to you, because I want you to do as I do. I'm letting you know how important My Word is. I want you to receive, and the manifestations shall keep coming to you, from Me.

**Let me tell you how awesome my God is. Listen to this word:** I've been through the storm and rain; through the Hurricane, but I made it. God brought me through. What He's done for me, He will do the same for you.

Trust Him and obey, because God has made a way, by grace through faith. Receive what He has to say.

Follow His instructions. Receive impartation, increase, and inspiration. He's allowed me to speak to the nation, helping this generation.

God put the fight in me. He changed my sorrow to joy. He dried my tears, and turned them into a smile. I believe I will stay in this place for a while. This is a place of triumph and not defeat.

God keeps on blessing me. What the enemy meant for bad, He allowed it to be for my good. In the storm I stood. Now I'm stronger than ever before. God has opened every door. I receive more and more. More than I had before.

No Hurricane can stop me; from God, I will never flee. Look what God has done for me. My family is with me, closer and closer we continue to be. We have been rescued. See what God can and will do.

You see us now, and you say "Wow!" How He did it all? I don't know how. Only God can and always will bring us out!

Some people were afraid to call, however God allowed the call. Some didn't understand, but God keeps allowing us to stand. Standing strong, in and through the storm.

Some days were challenging, however I praised Him anyway. God allowed the blessings to keep coming our way. Every day, I continued to pray. There were days I didn't know what to say.

I knew I had to keep moving at all times. I had to keep God on my mind. There were good days and bad ones. Because of God's son, I have won. In Christ Jesus this is where I am, and this is what I've become. I've been blessed in-spite of the mess.

God has allowed me to be His Messenger, with a message to tell. I shall never take for granted what He's placed in me. This message I shall continue to speak.

All those who will hear, know that in God there's no fear. Obedience is the key. Pay close attention to me! Listen up! Never give in to what the devil will do. Stay focused on the one and only true and living God. He will never leave or forsake you.

Sometimes, a word comes from people that you might not think are hearing God as you do. God put His Word in my oldest sister (Juanita) in times of her consoling me. Again she said, "You're gonna come through, this is a testimony for your book!"

I didn't know at that time, or even think she knew what she was saying. I just said, "I receive."

Of course, I asked God what He wanted me to do. Sometimes, things seem strange, but I began to hear God like never before. I prayed in the Spirit as I do every day. I asked Holy Spirit to speak to me concerning the things of God.

I prayed, "Lord allow your will to be done."

I'm happy in Christ Jesus, even in writing at this time. Praise, praise, and praise, is what I continue to do. Bishop William Murphy's praise songs take me into a praise with God like never before. I thank God for using him to bless the body of Christ and those that don't know Him at this time.

My prayer for those that don't know God yet is that they will receive Him, now! Ask God to forgive you for your sins, and come into your heart and save you now. Speak out loud, and remember this scripture:

> If you openly declare that Jesus is Lord and believe in your heart that God raised him from the dead, you will be saved.
>
> For it is by believing in your heart that you are made right with God, and it is by openly declaring your faith that you are saved.
>
> For everyone who calls on the name of the Lord will be saved.
>
> **Romans 10:9-10, 13 NLT**

I didn't understand at first why I couldn't sleep. Every two hours I would be wide-awake. I know now it was for God's sake. My daughter Tange said, "You're waking up like my three month old Josiah is doing for his feedings." I just laughed at her, and I realized it was true.

Now I see what God wanted me to do. I thank God for allowing me to keep writing to you. This isn't just for you, but for me too.

Storms come and they go. Why, where, and when, we don't know. The test is in the ships. Relationships. Where you dock. What you allow to come about. You can't control the current — God does. You can control where and how you land or end up. You can say enough is enough, "I don't want to go through this stuff."

You can choose to go through, or stop in the middle of the madness. I say, go through, because there's a message in the madness. Thank you Lord! I hope this message is blessing you as it's blessing me.

Keep listening, hearing, and doing. The blessing is in the moving. Keep moving. Don't stop until you get there.

*Water-Breaking Faith*

---

I had things to do every day, to handle things from the aftermath of the Hurricane, which definitely brought a change. I chose to keep doing it all in Jesus! At first I felt like I had lost it all: my clothes, shoes, household items, and precious things. I knew these were things I would get back, and more. I didn't allow those things to get me off track.

People would say to me, "It's just material things," I thought to myself, but they were all mine. I appreciated and knew they were trying to comfort me, but at that time I didn't want to hear it. If they found themselves in this position, I wondered, would they say and think the same thing? It's so easily said, when you're sleeping in your own bed. We were staying at a hotel, with five people in one room.

I thank God that all of us were together and no one was missing. We are all alive; we survived. God was, and is still, our guide.

My husband was on the rooftop, signaling for the boats to rescue us. My daughter Tange, and her two children Maranda and Josiah and I were all there with him. God came through.

My sister Shirley reached out on Facebook, and called and left a message pleading for someone to rescue us. Those people came from Dallas, Texas because of that voice message. Praise God!

I'm here today, writing so you can hear what God wants me to say. Each day is a new day, which I never take for granted. Each day gets better, even with stormy weather.

I'm choosing to cherish family and friends, even more. We never know when we have to walk through that door. I try to make sure I'm keeping focus. Sometimes, I don't feel like it though. I just want things to go back to where they were before the hurricane.

I know now that God brought about this change. God brought us out of the mess to receive His very best, because as His children we are far greater than the rest.

I said to God, "Thank you, for what I went through." This has made me stronger, even though it looked like things were no longer.

Our family and friends that truly loved us came through, but the fake ones, God will show them to you.

I have removed people from my space, that shouldn't have been there anyway. People that we thought would call or reach out but didn't. Some delayed calling because they didn't know what to say.

I say thanks again to all my loved ones who supported, said comforting words, and sent financial blessings. I know now what people in disasters have been through. I thank God He allows me to be a Messenger with a message. He's sent me, because I'm willing to go and tell my testimony.

Here I am awake at 3 a.m. I'm listening to more praise and worship songs. These songs take me into God's presence like never before. I know He's opened every door.

I'm so thankful always for what's He's done and continues to do in my life. I never have to guess what He keeps saying, and has said. God continues to speak to me in Psalms and hymns and spiritual songs, as I make melodies in my heart unto Him.

God has blessed us again, as we continue to win. We are almost out of the hotel now, and about to move into our new home. We purchased new furniture, even without a contract on the home. We continue to walk by faith and not by sight. We know that with Him we can never loose sight, as we continue to love God with all our might.

I'm proud and amazed as my husband keeps on going, even in the not knowing. He's been inspirational throughout this process, as we continue progress, and receive God's provision for our lives. We survived. Thank you Lord!

Again, I'm so grateful to God for bringing us through the storm and rain, from this Hurricane. As we continue in Christ Jesus, we remain. Our lives will never be the same. I praise His holy name. God is wonderful to me. He's set me here for all the world to see. I say look at what He's done. Victory, victory, victory, we have won, all because of His son!

In Christ Jesus I remain. I'm confident, compassionate, and in control. Where He leads me, I will go, even when I don't know. I have faith to trust and believe, all things through him, I shall behold, as these places and things unfold.

I'm expecting great things to manifest, even in this mess. This mess that man made. When the reservoirs were released, then came the flood waters that I thought would never cease.

They said this had to be done, however people were told to stay in their homes. Some area residents had mandatory evacuations and some did not. I wonder who's in control of what we got?

We worked hard at building up our lives, and being comfortable in our homes. Then one day the storm came, and our homes were gone. Flooded. Who's to blame? They say the Hurricane. This question still remains.

Again, our lives will never be the same. Memories, we will not forget, with God we forgive, because this is how we choose to live. We know satan has his place, but our God never makes a mistake. Some things have to happen, receive where He wants you to be.

I know that God doesn't make bad things happen, but He allows them to come. We have to keep living in His son. Christ Jesus is the only way. Keep living for him every day. Each day gets better; we've survived the stormy weather. What can I say? God keeps making a way out of no way.

We keep living by faith. Don't loose heart, and remember who's been with you from the start. He will never depart.

When my heart is overwhelmed, I pray, I stay, and I obey what God has to say. I move out of the way.

I thank God for my daughter Tange, as she cares for her two children, Maranda and Josiah. She never shows them discouragement, only encouragement. Even when things are not as she wants them to be right now, she knows God has brought her out.

Favor, keeps coming, as we keep going and sowing. There's no stopping us. We are Gods best, we keep passing all tests. He's made us far greater than the rest — we are His very best.

In Christ Jesus, you can be where you want to be. You can speak what you want and not what you don't want. Check these scripture out!

> You will also decide and decree a thing, and it will be established for you; And the light [of God's favor] will shine upon your ways.
> **Job 22:28 AMP**

> Now tell them this: 'As surely as I live, declares the Lord, I will do to you the very things I heard you say.
> **Numbers 14:28 NLT**

I'm encouraged and I try not to be discouraged. I'm amazed at what God allows to keep coming our way!

Friends and family keep blessing us as we continue to keep moving into God's provision, promotions, and promises He's provided for us. People we never imagined would bless us, they did. It's not about us, however. People are obedient to what they hear God say.

I praise God! This is a praise break moment! I'm listening to Lies, by Bishop William Murphy! Shouting now! He says, "The devil is a lair!"

What the Lord has is for me. "I'm going to stay here; I refuse to be run away." Praise God! Shouting now! Bless God! Get the CD!!! See you soon! Be back in a moment! Praise Him with me!!! Ok, I'm back; I'm in tack! It's quite all right to take a praise break! Praise gets God attention!

> The Spirit is God's guarantee that he will give us the inheritance he promised and that he has purchased us to be his own people. He did this so we would praise and glorify him.
> **Ephesians 1:14 NLT**

**This is what God spoke to me about praising Him:** When we praise God continually, we have favor with all people, and souls are added continually to the Church. When we praise God, money keeps on coming. When we praise God, seeds keeps on coming. When we praise God, healing keeps on coming. When we praise God, ministry keeps on flourishing. When we praise God, manifestations keeps on flooding. When we praise God, miracles keeps on flowing. When we praise God, marriages keep on growing. When we praise God, minds keep on mediating.

When we praise God, everywhere we look His love is still around. When we praise God, we hear the sound. When we praise God, the reign comes down. When we praise God, we are no longer bound. When we praise God, the lost souls are found. When we praise God, satan's kingdom drowns. When we praise God, His Kingdom reigns.

When we praise God, His blessings remain. When we praise God, we are connected to His Holy Spirit, in Jesus' name. When we praise God, nothing remains the same. When we praise God, He teaches us how to walk. When we praise God, He changes the way we talk. When we praise God, we receive blessings everywhere we walk. When we praise God, satan's kingdom falls. When we praise God, we receive everything we call.

When we praise God, we have a new song. When we praise God, we worship Him all day long. When we praise God, we shout because He allows everything to come about. When we praise God, our enemies are defeated and destroyed. When we praise God, we are full of joy.

When we praise God, doors are opened. When we praise God, doors that we opened are shut. When we praise God, we enter into His place of rest, because He's given us His very best: Christ Jesus has cleaned us up from all our mess.

When we praise God, we receive far greater than the rest, and we pass every test. When we praise God, we obey what He has said, is saying, and continues to say. When we praise God, all His promises keep coming our way, and they are here to stay.

When we praise God, we are restored, ruling, reigning, resting, remaining, and receiving, all His revelations every day. When we praise God, we continue to pray.

When we praise God, we hear, listen, and do what Holy Spirit speaks through us at all times. When we praise God, we shine in His divine, every time, and all these blessings are mine. When we praise God, He is always near. When we praise God, we recognize the enemy, and we have no fear.

When we praise God, our worship is for real. When we praise God, it's not about how we feel. When we praise God, we praise Him for who He is. When we praise God, we don't have to be asking Him for anything at that time, we praise Him because we love Him, and He's always on our mine.

When we praise God, from the inside out, He rewards us openly. When we praise God, we worship Him in spirit and in truth. When we praise God, it's not hard to do, we just come saying God we love you!

### See these scriptures:

> Praising God continually, and having favor with all the people. And the Lord kept adding to their number daily those who were being saved.
>
> **Acts 2:47 AMP**

> Then King Jehoshaphat bowed low with his face to the ground. And all the people of Judah and Jerusalem did the same, worshiping the Lord.
>
> At the very moment they began to sing and give praise, the Lord caused the armies of Ammon, Moab, and Mount Seir to start fighting among themselves.

> Then all the men returned to Jerusalem, with Jehoshaphat leading them, overjoyed that the Lord had given them victory over their enemies.
>
> **2 Chronicles 20:18, 22, 27 NLT**

It's another day to glorify and praise God! I'm getting started with my day; let's see what God has brought our way. Keep reading. I know you're being blessed. You are God's very best. I speak this to you today. Trust God. Do what He says. Always abide in Him, as this scripture tells us:

> If you remain in Me and My words remain in you [that is, if we are vitally united and My message lives in your heart], ask whatever you wish and it will be done for you.
>
> **John 15:7 AMP**

Today is a great day. Let's see what He allows to come our way! Rising early is a blessing. Just being able to rise is a blessing also. Seek Him early. Never miss the message, in His Messenger.

> "And they rose early in the morning, and went forth into the wilderness of Tekoa: and as they went forth, Jehoshaphat stood and said, Hear me, O Judah, and ye inhabitants of Jerusalem; Believe in the Lord your God, so shall ye be established; believe his prophets, so shall ye prosper."
>
> **2 Chronicles 20:20 KJV**

Sleeping is important, but early rising is also. Don't dream to long, and be left alone. Hear what God has to say, get up early and know how to start your day. Here I am up early!

**Listen up!**

The gates are open and we drive in to this large space of this large place. This place that's too large to walk in, that's why we drive in. This place where we continue to win.

We follow God with all our hearts. We will never depart, because He's set us apart. We are in. We don't follow in darkness, and in light we follow God with all our might, money, and manifestation, because He's always on our mind. From mind time, to money and manifestation time. We are in line as we walk, and shine in God's divine.

Hurricane Harvey tried to take us out, however we continued to shout, because He's the one that brought us all out. It's our mission to keep walking with God's permission, because He's placed us in this position.

Our Ministry has taken on new life and a new way of living, because of our giving. We love, and live to give, and our life in Christ Jesus is for real.

God says vengeance is His, and He shall repay. People will watch what they say, and they will do what God says, when it comes to blessing us in every way. The blessings just keep on coming our way, even today. I receive, and I thank You Lord for every day, and what You allow to keep coming our way.

Shake, shake, shake, God has allowed an earthquake. This is a shaking up of money and exploding into our hands and bank accounts. The money is given because our heart's desire is to give.

God has provided, and keeps providing the seeds to sow into the soil, directed by His Holy Spirit. We are led and fed, all because of what we read. We have heard the word spoken by God's prophet, our Apostle, Dr. Leroy Thompson.

We remember the words, money with a mission. This money for the vision. Our vision will be carried out, because He's allowed it to come to pass, and it shall last.

We keep teaching and preaching lessons because we have been given a message. We follow the Trinity, and walk in His Divinity, as we have our identity. We follow instructions from His Holy Spirit, and we obey what's been spoken out; again, all His promises that He allows to keep coming about.

In Christ Jesus we have been given a message from the messenger. We praise God now as we continue to shout. God has spoken and our seeds have caused all curses to be broken. Poverty will never stand in the way of our prosperity another day in our lives.

We have the mind of Christ and we will never think broke again, because we have been made to always win. God will keep blessing us over and over again.

He's done it for our Apostle, Dr. Leroy Thompson, and He's done the same for us. We have received all blessings that have been spoken over us. Thank You God for it all.

We shall never fall or fail, because He's delivered our mail. Checks keep coming in. Life is great and we have received, because we do things for His kingdom sake, and He keeps making a way out of no way. The blessings just keep coming our way!

What we saw as a tragedy, God has caused us to triumph. Every situation isn't what we see at first, however we must keep looking to see what's at the end. The end is our destiny.

We must keep our hearts, minds, and ears clear, so we can continue to hear. What are we listening for? The sound and rhythm of the beat of abundance, for the kingdom and for me. Watch what you say. Why? God will do the very things He hears you say. Again see, Numbers 14:28 NLT.

Say what you want to come your way. Keep reading. Hear, listen, and do everything He speaks to you.

**Listen in!**

I am a sign and a wonder. God has given me everything. God has given me His plans of prosperity. My expected end is to win. I drive in. The gates are open. God has spoken. All the enemy's curses are broken.

My ups always outlast my downs. God is always around. I never have to frown. God has allowed me to smile even when the road gets rough. I'm built to last. I'm strong in the Lord and in the power

*The Journey Begins*

of His might. In Christ Jesus I never loose sight. I love God with all my might.

In the times of famine, I'm always satisfied with the fatness and fruits of the land. My finances increase every day. He's allowing this manifestation to keep coming my way. I obey everyday in every way.

My senses are tuned into His channels. My mind is alert to the things of God. I never fall or fail. I'm on track and making tracks. People follow me because I follow Him. I continue to speak God's Word, so people can speak His Word back to Him and receive their salvation.

**Read this scripture, speak out loud, and receive. Thank God!**

> "That if thou shalt confess with thy mouth the Lord Jesus, and shalt believe in thine heart that God hath raised him from the dead, thou shalt be saved."
>
> **Romans 10:9 KJV**

**Listen up!**

God's word is alive and in me. I see and say what He says. My speaking is in line with the light that shines through me. They see the God in me. My love for Him causes people to love Him.

Wisdom, wealth, and His Word are being heard. When I speak, wisdom speaks. My wealth causes people to see and receive His Word, which continues to be heard. Following instructions from Holy Spirit is the key to receive the keys to the Kingdom.

I'm no longer looking in from the outside; I live from the inside out. My inner man continues to stand. There's no struggle, stress, or strain. God has allowed me to gain and remain. My giving has reached new levels. I have power over devils.

I rule, rest, and reign. I never stop. Moving is key. Standing still won't help in the storm. I know where my help comes from. Action is not a fraction.

I never have to figure it out. God has already worked it out. I keep obeying, praying, and staying. In this place of promises, provisions, promotions, and prosperity, it's all for me. I receive it all by grace through faith.

Increase keeps coming my way. Increase is here to stay. I shall never stray. This Hurricane has brought my harvest. My seeds don't just meet my needs, they bring increase.

My desires are God desires for me. I'm connected to the harvest because of my seeds sown. I own. Wealthy place, I'm living in. Large place, I'm in. I've tipped over the scale. I have so much money, not enough room to receive. God has given and keeps giving, all this money to me.

The Kingdom of God is at hand. The Kingdom of God shall continue to stand. I'm open to receive all that God has for me. I Receive Now! I thank you God!

My hands are anointed. Everything I touch increases. My hands are blessed; I will never receive mess. My hands are clean. My heart is pure. My service is to God and then I can serve man. It's all in His plans. I receive and follow instructions He has given me.

I reach, teach, and preach what God has given me. I never let go of what I know. He allows me to be a show.

Through my wealth, people will see God in my life. They pay attention to His goodness, and want to know what to do to receive, as He's blessed me.

I never gave into what I went through. I had no doubt that God would bring me out. We were rescued! Look at what God can do, and has done. I keep praising! Even right now, I'm shouting as I'm writing! To God be the glory! For all the things He's done! I have won. I have victory because of His son!

Today is another day. Dreams keep coming my way. Good ones and bad ones. I know the bad one comes to fix what's been broken. The good ones are to receive what God has spoken.

I'm never sleep on the enemy. I know he wants to stop me. I keep pressing, with the message.

*The Journey Begins*

We received favor on yesterday from The Lutheran Church, just outside of Chicago, Illinois. Who would have thought these people would come from our hometown of Chicago? These were believers who volunteered their services to help us with the next phase of repairing our home.

We also received favor from the Latter Day Saints, in Spring, Texas with the first phase, which was cleaning out and gutting our home. The Lutheran Church, from Spring, Texas came to finish the next phase where the others left off. God is awesome!

Today, I was looking back at what I went through again. I was sad at first, then God began to allow His Holy Spirit to minister to me. Thank you Lord! Again, I've received more than I had before! On satan, I immediately shut the door.

Your mind has to stay focused on the now. Allow God to keep showing you how. Stay focused, and in faith. See what God allows to keep coming your way! Pray, and stay, every day!

Keep praising, even in what you see as bad times. Even when things look like they are out of line. Remember we shine in His divine, all the time. God is great and greatly to be praised, I bless His Holy name.

Again, my life will never be the same. In Christ Jesus, I remain. I didn't just survive; I'm here because God kept me alive. I was made to subdue, replenish, and multiply.

> "And God blessed them, and God said unto them, Be fruitful, and multiply, and replenish the earth, and subdue it: and have dominion over the fish of the sea, and over the fowl of the air, and over every living thing that moveth upon the earth."
>
> **Genesis 1:28 KJV**

I'm excited to see what today will bring! In Christ Jesus, I receive everything! We have the estimates for repairs to our home.

We believe favor has found us. We won't pay what the estimates say. Favor has allowed the best price to come our way.

Money is freed, for our next seed! Thank you Lord! We continue to sow our way out. This is how God allows the favor to keep coming about. Seed time and harvest time never cease, regardless of what we see. Money keeps on coming to me! Thank you Lord!

I'm up early again, listening to praise and worship songs, getting ready to tap into His presence, where we always win! I will receive and let you listen in. Okay, make sure you hear what God has to say today. This is what He's spoken. Get ready to step out and into your large place He's set for us. Are you ready? I am. Let's go!

# Water Breaking Faith!

*This is a very important part of this book! This explains more of why this Title is key! See what He's spoken to me!*

This faith comes with favor that pushes you out of famine and into fruitfulness, and finances that flood in with face value. God has given us the vindication and set us before the nation. People will see it straight in their face. They will say, "Look what God has done. Victory has been won, because of His son!"

We have value. People see our worth, spiritually and physically. We are led by the Spirit. We are connected with Holy Spirit and in this physical body.

God uses us to be a blessing, as we have been made a blessing. We are blessed going out and blessed coming in. We are blessed in the cities and blessed in the fields. The harvest has come. We receive. Thank you Lord.

We didn't have to go far. The harvest was always near. We had no fear. We moved close to the place where we once lived before Hurricane Harvey. Why? The blessing was always near. God blesses you close to where you are. The land had already been searched and traveled on. Every place the soles of our feet tread is ours.

> Every place whereon the soles of your feet shall tread shall be yours: from the wilderness and Lebanon, from

> the river, the river Euphrates, even unto the uttermost sea shall your coast be.
>
> **Deuteronomy 11:24 KJV**

Go back to the place where we have been. It's waiting for us to step in. It's already been prepared, by grace, through faith. We have Water Breaking Faith.

Go God's way! Pay close attention to the gates that swing open. You will drive in. The doors are too small. Look for the place that you have called. What you've called has come to pass. Go back and mediate, get your mind in motion to receive the manifestation that's been made and moved into your marriage, ministry, and money.

Don't say God hasn't showed you where, it has always been there waiting on you to drive into. Go back and revisit the place where you said you couldn't afford. Now! Never speak out of your mouth what you can't afford ever again. You have been pushed out of poverty and into prosperity.

The water came in Jesus' name. "I gave my permission," says our almighty God! "Nothing comes to my people without my permission." Just like with Job; God gave satan permission to take his possessions, and said don't touch him. See this scripture:

> "Then the LORD said to Satan, "Behold, all that Job has is in your power, only do not put your hand on the man himself." So Satan departed from the presence of the LORD."
>
> **Job 1:12 AMP**

"You have experienced the pains, pushing, and now I have pleasure in prospering you," says Almighty God! You would not have given birth without the water breaking! You have made your last push. Your blessings have come through! The deliverance of blessings is here. Everywhere you go, blessings are in the atmosphere!

Receive. Say right now, out your mouth, "I receive. Thank God for blessing me!" Praise Him now!

Favor will keep coming, even when you don't know how, right now. Loaded, large, limitless, finances are flooding, flowing, and following favor now. Receive. I receive now.

"Continue to keep the faith, trust and believe. I have made all these blessings to keep coming your way," says Almighty, All-powerful God!

Water breaking Faith can't be stopped. The birthing of blessings had to come out. Just like the babies can't come without the water breaking. God has set the bar, without a top. No limits. You are in. You will see your expected end. You needed the assistance of the hurricane to receive in Jesus name! The plans that have been set up for you, you must drive in! This is a command. It's in your hands. Believe, and receive. Thank God!

As I sit here today, I'm still rejoicing from what God keep allowing to come our way! Last week was favor after favor finding us again! The Lutheran Church came through again! Our house was treated for mold. We met other amazing believers, who volunteered their time and service again to help us with the repair process. We are absolutely grateful to God for sending them, and they obeyed Him in assisting us.

I received a call the next day from the Lutheran Church, asking if we needed more help. More favor! Favor comes before the finances! This favor causes us to free up more money to keep sowing our seeds in good soil, and keep receiving more favor. Praise God! Glory hallelujah! Glory to God! He gets the highest praise! I Bless His name!

The church volunteers came out to measure for drywall and use our home as a model to see how to help others with their repairs. Thank God! "Favor just keeps on coming, and the money just keeps on coming!" says Apostle Dr. Leroy Thompson. Every time we sow our seed, we continue to receive favor, and finances, immediately.

People will watch what they say about what has come our way. Speak no evil. Vengeance, God will repay.

People will begin to come from the north, south, east, and the west to be a part of God's very best. Believers will hear God like never before, they will know who has opened all doors. Unbelievers will turn from their way of living, and ask to be forgiven. Backsliders will repent and turn back to God's way of living. People will be reconciled back to Him. Believers will hear, listen, and do, all that's been commanded of them to do.

**Check out these passages of scriptures:**

> "He will repay his enemies for their evil deeds. His fury will fall on his foes. He will pay them back even to the ends of the earth. In the west, people will respect the name of the Lord; in the east, they will glorify him. For he will come like a raging flood tide driven by the breath of the Lord. "The Redeemer will come to Jerusalem to buy back those in Israel who have turned from their sins," says the Lord. "And this is my covenant with them," says the Lord. "My Spirit will not leave them, and neither will these words I have given you. They will be on your lips and on the lips of your children and your children's children forever. I, the Lord, have spoken!"
>
> **Isaiah 59:18-21 NLT**

God is no respecter of persons, what He's done for others He will do the same for you. We are truly blessed to be a blessing. God is causing people to obey, and do for us what He says. Our friends — notice I said friends, not just people who want to know what's going on with us and aren't really concerned. They have been a blessing, and continue to bless. Not just in word, but in deed.

Financially! Thank God! Stay tuned! Keep listening in! See what tomorrow brings!

Today, God keeps allowing the blessings to keep coming our way! Thank you Lord! The repairs of the drywall started today. As I sit and listen to Chris Tomlin — Good Good Father — I'm grateful for the people who are helping in the repairs. People have come from Nebraska to help. I was told there were some ladies that were great at helping with the drywall. Our house is being repaired with the spirit of excellency.

I'm enjoying the awesome and caring spirit of the people assisting us. We are never bothered by the crowd; we want God to be proud. He is pleased in the prosperity of His servants. He's made the way; it's already done, by grace through faith.

You will hear me keep repeating this. We shall remain in faith, all the way! Nothing stops our faith. Thank God for His amazing grace! As the testimonies continue to build, we continue to stay in God's will.

Our mind is made up. We are not crying over stuff. Even though the road gets rough. I know God is ruling, I rest, and receive all that He's restored to me. I shall recover all, regardless of what I've seen fall.

We have the victory over the enemy. What he meant for bad, God gave us more than what we had. Thank you Lord!

God has blessed me to write more than one book at a time. He allows me to share with you what He's put on my mind. I shine in His divine! Everything I speak is for these times.

As I continue to pray in the spirit, He speaks revelations in these real times. We must remember that faith is believing and trusting in what God speaks, not what you choose to believe on your own. If He speaks it, He's obligated to give it to you. You must work in connection with His Holy Spirit, obey, and follow His instructions.

Have faith in Him, and no doubt. What you speak according to His will, you will receive.

> "Jesus replied, "Have faith in God [constantly]. I assure you and most solemnly say to you, whoever says to this mountain, 'Be lifted up and thrown into the sea!' and does not doubt in his heart [in God's unlimited power], but believes that what he says is going to take place, it will be done for him [in accordance with God's will]. For this reason I am telling you, whatever things you ask for in prayer [in accordance with God's will], believe [with confident trust] that you have received them, and they will be given to you."
>
> **Mark 11:22-24 AMP**

Know that when stepping out and you don't know what, or have anything to step onto, just believe that God will give it to you if you ask. I pump up my praise every day. I ask Holy Spirit to lead me in every way. I never want to go astray.

I purpose in my heart to obey what God says. I love Him so. I've received my comfortable place of praise again. Where I'm living, He's given. It's important to have that special place to hear from God.

I'm dancing like David danced. I have my songs of praise. I bless His Holy name! I Receive in Jesus' name!

**The Shine Is On! You Have Won!**

Good morning all. Here's what God spoke to me this early morning.

The candle of the Lord is burning bright. I've blessed you tonight. Many of your blessings have been put in the people's sight. You are on display. Continue to obey. All these blessings have come and shall continue to come your way.

The flame of the fire has burned up all the lack and not enough. You have received your stuff. The material things are not a dream anymore: they have been placed at your door.

Go open the door now, and let them in. When you open the door, say, "I receive my material blessings now, and I thank You Lord for them."

Remember when you do the ridiculous; you receive the miraculous! This is a miracle move form God to you! What you knew you couldn't afford, I have allowed you to receive. Because of your seeds, your supernatural surplus has blessed you indeed. It's all from me. Tell them you are sent by God, they will receive.

Holy Ghost fire fall on the great and small. Your BIG has come in. Reach in. Receive the money in the fish mouth. I've brought you out. Shout! Praise Me without any doubt. Again I've brought this all about.

I'm your almighty God! Listen, hear, and do what I've spoken. Financial curses have been broken. Sow big! Permit Holy Spirit to show you how to dig deeper depths and higher heights. Sow with all your might.

You got the power to get the wealth. Prosperity is your birthright. Never lose sight. People will say, "Look at what the Lord has done, it's marvelous in our sight!"

Beyond breakthrough, that's you! It's all for you! "It's My pleasure," says the almighty God!

Rejoice and be exceedingly glad, you have more money than you ever had. Money that keeps on coming! Continue to keep the faith; it's already done by grace, through faith. You have favor, stay focused; your finances are flooding, flourishing, and flowing. Now!

As we are repairing our home, we stop and see what's needed to complete the process. We say, "Wow, so much more is needed."

While the drywall was being completed, I was asked what type of floors I wanted to put in. I responded, "I haven't thought about it yet." I told the people, "I have faith and believe and trust God all the way. He will continue to send blessings my way." At the time, I had no idea where the monies would come from. Laughing now! All I know is, God said, "He's made me a show." He shows off in me. The blessings keep coming to me!

Good morning! Allow me to paint this picture, before I share this message today of what God showed me and gave me the interpretation. Here we go!

Today as I lay in bed with my eyes still closed, this is what God showed me.

God took me to a higher level. As I was looking down, I couldn't see the ground. God said, "I've raised you up, away from the crazy stuff, you shall receive much."

There were certain things I had to be removed from before He could place me into where I needed to be. I'm soaring like an eagle. I'm no longer walking or running. My destiny is near. I have no fear of what I hear.

Negative people, and things, I can't and won't receive. I believe, I trust, and I have faith that God has done it all by grace through my faith. He continues to allow everything to come my way. Today is a great day.

Things will happen for us today that will give us an Awe experience! We will be amazed at the awesome things God keeps giving. We keep giving because we know this: so is Jesus, so are we. We love like He loves, from heaven above. With this love we are harmless as doves.

God loves us so, He gave His only begotten son. With His love He allowed His son to die, and come out of the grave. Because of His love, and our love for Him, we obey. We do what He says.

With His love, blessings will keep coming our way! Because of His love, I'm alive today! With His love, I can stay. In His presence, that's where I am. Why? Because He's the great I Am!

Giving, giving, giving, that's how we are living! He's ministered seed to the sower. We are sowers. We have purpose in our hearts to live set apart. That means Holy. That's who we are. God is never far. He's always near. No fear, but faith, power, love, and a sound mind.

We chose to leave no souls behind. Doing God's will is His Great Commission. We purpose in our hearts to help lost souls come into His Kingdom, and pray, prophesy, preach, and prepare the ones that are there. We have power and ability to get what God has released.

He's given us back all that the enemy has stolen. We have received. We give God Glory and thanks for all things He's done and continue to do, all because of His love.

We are free to live according to God's will. We are willing and obedient, and we receive the good of the land. It's all in His plans. See His plans below:

> For I know the plans and thoughts that I have for you,' says the LORD, 'plans for peace and well-being and not for disaster to give you a future and a hope."
> **Jeremiah 29:11 AMP**

As we continue in this process of repairs of our home. We are never alone. I keep speaking, and blessings just keep coming our way. Even today, great things are coming our way!

Again, God will do the very things He hears you say. Keep speaking what you want, and not what you don't want. Even when things look like they are not working in your favor, know that you have favor and faith to bring these things your way. Remember, God does what He hears you say.

We have peace that surpasses all our understanding. Peace that the Hurricane couldn't take. Harvey took things away. Our love, peace, and joy, is still full. God is still good! Real, real, good! God's grace, and mercy endures forever! We choose to rejoice and be exceedingly glad! He has given us more than we ever had!

See below what God said about what we went through, and how we came through, and now we are beyond breakthrough. This is a great book by Apostle Dr. Leroy Thompson. I'm not marketing anyone's books, I'm just informing you on my process, and charting the course of my experiences, as the Title says, **Water-Breaking Faith.**

> "You know we call those blessed [happy, spiritually prosperous, favored by God] who were steadfast and endured [difficult circumstances]. You have heard of the patient endurance of Job and you have seen the Lord's outcome [how He richly blessed Job]. The Lord is full of compassion and is merciful."
>
> **James 5:11 AMP**

Praise break now! I'm shouting! Wow! Listening to Bishop William Murphy, be Gloried! To God be the glory! Keep your eyes on the Lord, regardless of what you see! We must take pleasure in the finished works God has prepared for us!

> Rejoice in the Lord always [delight, take pleasure in Him]; again I will say, rejoice!
>
> **Philippians 4:4 AMP**

Again, today is a great day! Family day! Picnic time! This is a day of enjoying family. It's important. Last night was movie night. Enjoy your children, and grandchildren. I know this is blessing you. Some people don't even like their family or get along with them. Let's change that today.

Do things God's way. Love starts at home first, then spreads everywhere else. This is my prayer now! Continue reading on, as I

*Water-Breaking Faith!*

allow God to keep showing me how. I'm blessing Him now, for what He's doing in your life even right now. Thank God for change!

**This is what I speak daily and you can too.**

I permit you Holy Spirit to reveal to me in the spirit, so that I'm always Spirit led and Spirit fed. Holy Spirit show me how, when, where, who, and what to do to obey God in every area of my life, so that I will receive of Him on this earth, and others will receive of Him as well, through me.

**November 7, 2017 @ 6:45 a.m.**

Keep sowing; the seeds are coming in. I've made you a sower. I have ministered seeds to you, now you know what to do. Don't think the seeds are for you. You will have your time to dine in my divine. Your shine is the next time. Seed time and harvest time shall never cease when you obey Me. Hear Me and do as I say.

Money will keep coming your way. Money is here to stay. Never do things your way. I've brought you out, now Shout!

I've made you a millionaire. Be prepared, money will come to you from everywhere.

Your favor awaits you when you return home. Your new church property has been released. Your short delay was all about My favor without labor.

People will ask you what can they do to help you build up the Kingdom. Don't think it's strange, they will come in Jesus' name, saying God sent them. You will know because of the seeds they will sow.

Training is a must for them to receive their stuff. They have been asking Me for things they desire, this is how they shall acquire, because the seeds I require. The kingdom prospers with the seeds; beggars are always in need. You don't have to plead, just receive.

Again, I've released the seeds. All needs are met. Your money has broken the nets. You have already reached in and gotten the money out of the fish mouth. Praise Me with a loud shout.

Walls are down, because you have walked around. I've commissioned and you have My permission to go yea therefore and bring people into the doors that I've opened. I've made an open show out of you. What people see will draw them to Me. I draw them all to Me now, never worry about how. They will drink from the well that never runs dry. No more drought it's drinking time.

Shine now in My divine. It's your time. I am the Almighty God of all. Keep following My instructions you will never fall.

Even in our darkest hour we still have power. This strength, authority, and might we will never lose sight. As we continue to follow God's instructions, and allow Holy Spirit to assist us in all that we do: God has already made it all happen for us, I say again, we win! We are led by His spirit within.

We hear from God like never before. We are not just entering into doors, we are entering into gates, and we drive in. The time has come to soar. We are eagles. God's love is the highest level. We have power over devils. No evil can defeat us. We are never destroyed; we are destined to reach our divine destination.

Again, we have been set before the nations. People see what God wants us to be. We have been made an open show. God shows His goodness through us.

Resting in His promises, as we continue to receive. He's already met our needs. Our desires are in line, and we shine in His divine, all the time. I receive, all His promises that have been given me! Blessing, blessing, I receive, as I decree.

Lessons, I've learned in His presence, as I continue to be. As God continue to speak to me, by way of His Holy Spirit. My ears are always open to the messages that keep coming to me. I see what He wants, and not just where He wants me to be.

In the spirit, my eyes are always open. Life looks great! People are running from everywhere to be a part of His Kingdom that has come. God's will is being done. His people obey, what He says.

The Great Commission is being carried out. People come in with a shout. God has brought them out. Out of poverty into prosperity! We have learned prosperity is our birthright. Apostle Dr. Leroy Thompson spoke this at the 2017 Prosperity Revival. We believe and we receive our prosperity!

Today is Tuesday, my husband, Pastor AD, told me about how God spoke to him, and he responded and did what He said. Our seeds continue to work for us, because God ministers seed to the sower. We continue to sow our way out, and into our wealthy place.

We are His chosen generation, we are blessed, and He's set us in this large place, before the nations. Money just keeps on coming to us. My husband obeyed God on Tuesday and by Friday, we received thousands of dollars that we didn't know we had coming. God reminded me again, that He would give us money we didn't know about, as we continue to sow our way out. Thank you Lord!!!

Apostle Leroy Thompson told us, "This will be the best Christmas you have ever had." We believed and received that word, and we are prospering. I'm choosing to chart the course, and allowing you to see what our awesome and almighty God has done because of our obedience in following His instructions.

Remember, Hurricane Harvey did it's part, as he stole from us and tried to destroy what God had given us. We shall continue doing our part in building up God's Kingdom and what God has done, and He keeps on making a way out of no way for us. We are enjoying life, and receiving exceedingly and abundantly, above all that we could have ever asked or thought of.

> "The thief cometh not, but that he may steal, and kill, and destroy: I came that they may have life, and may have it abundantly."
>
> **John 10:10 KJV**

We are buying our families nice gifts for Christmas. In past years we were not able to spend a nice amount of money on them. To God be the glory!

It's Friday and we are headed to Orlando, Florida, to set sail on Saturday for our one-week cruise.

It's Sunday on the cruise, and we have received favor. God is showing us how His Kingdom children live. The Director of the cruise has given us favor, and people are serving us. Glory to God! Thank you Lord!

After the storm, this is a much-needed cruise. I can't wait to hear and see what God does next! I know that I'm His very elect, and He's given, and keeps on giving, me His very best! Praise God! Stay tuned! See you next time!

See how He allows me to shine! God has made us an open show! I praise God for your time, even if you don't know. You might experience a hurricane. If so, I know your life will never be the same. Keep the faith, and do everything God's way. Follow His instructions. God needs you to stay connected to the Vine. Stay in line. God can't do it for you, except if you participate with Him. There's always a cause and effect.

**Cause:** Because you are willing and obedient,
**Effect:** You shall eat the good of the land.

> If you are willing and obedient, You shall eat the best of the land;
>
> **Isaiah 1:19 AMP**

**Today is Tuesday of our cruise:** As I have stepped out onto the balcony of our cabin, I began to look across the waters, which looked like it would never end. I looked to the left, right, up, and down, then I closed my eyes. I prayed in the Holy Ghost while my eyes were closed. With my head facing up, and my eyes closed, I saw a very bright light. While my eyes were still closed and my head was facing straight ahead, I saw all red. I opened my eyes and I noticed the ship was allowing people to disembark across a connecting walk that allowed them to go tour Jamaica. I then came back into my cabin.

**As I sat quietly and began to listened, the Holy Ghost began to speak this:** When I look out into God's creation, I see His marvelous works: water, skies, ships, and dry land. Looking up and closing my eyes, I see the bright light that God allowed me to be. My light so shines that people see it and He gets the glory. Looking ahead, closing my eyes, and seeing red, God says: "You're covered by the blood of Jesus."

I know I'm made in His image, as Jesus is the light of the world. Because of him I shine in His divine, all the time. Without the connection of Holy Spirit, I can't cross over to the land that flows with milk and honey, and plenty of money. This is a good land, a land of brooks and hills, where all my dreams are fulfilled.

This life is for real. Be still, and know that I'm God. I'm never far; I will not depart. Keep Me in your heart.

Keep His light shinning, keep the connection of Holy Spirit, listen, and pay close attention to what I hear, what I see, and all that's been revealed to me. Never try to cross over on the wrong side of the exit to dry land without the Holy Spirit's guidance. He will always lead me in the right direction, and I will always make it to my destination: all because of my connection.

This place I've entered into is a placed of dominion, deserving, and drinking. I have received the favor, fatness, fruitfulness, flooding, flowing, and finances of the land.

Never take for granted where I've been planted. My crops have come up. It's harvest time. Don't stop sowing seeds. Seed time and harvest time never cease.

My job in the Kingdom is to always increase. Increase in giving, living, and receiving. I'm an open show for all the world to see how God continues to bless me. I testify to how He's allowed my fruits, and my finances to remain and multiply.

God is no respecter of persons, what He's done for me, He will do the same for you. We must obey, and follow His instructions.

This hurricane came in the eighth month, and brought about a new beginning, now I'm winning. My husband, my children, my grandchildren and I are all alive. We didn't just survive; we have arrived. Where? This large place of rest, restoration, and receiving, of all God promises, provisions, promotions, and prosperity! Why? Because it gives Him pleasure! **This is the word from our almighty God!**

As I sit here on my balcony, I look out over the water and see what looks like never-ending waters. I know there's an ending or dry land out there somewhere, and I see an example of faith. Faith is knowing that there's an ending or destination beyond what I see. I believe that I will make it to my destination. I have to travel the paths it takes to get there, without doubting, obeying and following the instructions to the route.

The ship has a compass, therefore it won't get lost and have us sailing to the wrong destination. Orlando Florida is our destination on tomorrow. I believe and trust Norweign to take us there. I have faith in God to follow Holy Spirit's leadership to take me everywhere He wants me to be. In the scriptures, Jesus says take up your cross and follow me.

> "Then he said to the crowd, "If any of you wants to be my follower, you must give up your own way, take up your cross daily, and follow me."
>
> **Luke 9:23 NLT**

Favor just keeps on coming to me. We had favor in the purchases of diamonds and watches we desired while on the islands. Things that we thought we couldn't afford in the past, we now own, all because of the seeds we have sown. Money we sowed in building up the Kingdom of God. He's pleased. How do I know? He has pleasure in prosperity of His servants.

> Let them shout for joy, and be glad, that favour my righteous cause: yea, let them say continually, Let the Lord be magnified, which hath pleasure in the prosperity of his servant.
>
> **Psalms 35:27 KJV**

Obedience, instructions, and revelations are key, to receive your prosperity! In this book, I remind you that the water had to break in order to move us from our past situations and into our present status. Our future looks better than what we saw before. God says go yea therefore.

> Go ye therefore, and teach all nations, baptizing them in the name of the Father, and of the Son, and of the Holy Ghost:
>
> **Matthew 28:19 KJV**

We receive money for the Kingdom, and money just keeps on coming to us. It's not just about stuff. Things come to us, and we don't have to chase the things down. Now we have received the revelation of what Apostle Leroy Thompson taught us, "God is a giver."

I'm reminded of what God spoke in my book *The Secrets Are Out*, **"We will receive money that we didn't know was coming."** *It has happened!*

We shall continue following the instructions God has given us to continue this journey. Destinations are evident and we have received the evidence. Now Faith is the substance of things hoped for and the evidence of things we couldn't see. Now we see! Praise God for what He's given me!

Oh, how awesome is His name. No other name greater! We are truly blessed, and we are a blessing. I hear the water and see the waves, as we continue traveling on. Sounds like music in my ears. I have no fear. I have a sound mind; I love God all the time.

Power is what I have. Not that I didn't have it before the Hurricane, I just use it more after it came. What we see as bad things aren't always bad, some things had to come to remove, replace, and receive what God has already released. Thank you Lord!

Good morning! This is an early rising day for me, 4 a.m. I finished my spiritual workout, which is praying in the spirit while praise dancing and listening to more of Bishop William Murphy songs. This takes me into God's presence.

Worshipping God, and getting His attention, that's what worship does. This is what was revealed to me, after I was quiet, and listened. You must pay close attention and listen. You have to hear, listen, and do. After you pray, you must stay and see what God has to say, and revelations will come your way.

**This is what He revealed today. Thank you Lord!**

We're in a place that we've never been before. I see us walking through the open doors. The gates are open and we drive in. This is a place that we always win. We have permission, now; we enter in.

God's Holy Spirit keeps us hearing from within. This is the place that we always dreamed of. This is the place that's sent from heaven above. I'm in this place because of His love.

This place is where I live. This place is where I always give. In Christ Jesus I'm glad we met. It's never about what I can get. God is not done with me yet. What He's done, and keep doing, I will never forget.

I worship God in spirit and in truth. I allow Him to use me the way He wants to. I'm obedient to His Word. I'm hearing things I've never heard. I love God with all my heart. In this place He's positioned me; I will never depart. In this place He's never far. God will bless you where you are. In this place I've topped the bar.

My blessings are unlimited and lifetime. I'm shining in His divine. People are seeing what an awesome God I serve, all the glory He deserves! My life He has preserved. I Thank Him for it all! In this place I can't fall. I stay focused, and in faith. I keep doing things God's way. In this place I'm here to stay. Favor continues to find me every day; therefore, I will never stray.

His instructions I follow. I always have hope for today, and tomorrow. In this place I'm the lender, and not the borrower. In this place I have no sorrow.

At the cross Jesus paid it all. Thank God for the cross experience. In Him I have recompense. I Thank you Lord for the blood that was shed, and You allowing me to be Spirit led. My hope is in Christ Jesus.

I know I'm in this place for a reason. This is my due season. Seasons come and they go. Everywhere God leads me I will follow. Seasons are throughout the year. I continue to hear.

I got the power. I keep hearing, hour, after hour. Therefore, satan he can't devour this power I have. I tread over everything that tries to harm me.

> Behold, I give unto you power to tread on serpents and scorpions, and over all the power of the enemy: and nothing shall by any means hurt you.
>
> **Luke 10:19 KJV**

I'm not afraid of the devil. With this power, God has me on a higher level. Unlimited resources and revenue have been given to me. I continue to receive revelations, therefore I will help this generation, and generations to come. God's work never ceases to be done. We have won, because of His son, our savior. Don't stop. Keep seeking the Kingdom of God and His righteousness, and all things are added unto you. This is what I do.

> But seek ye first the kingdom of God, and his righteousness; and all these things shall be added unto you.
> **Matthew 6:33 KJV**

You will never have to chase after these things; they will find you. Keep obeying, and following the instructions God keeps giving you. He will always come through. In Him there's no failure.

I have been through the stormy weather. Remember the key word is "been" through. Now I'm writing this to you. Water-breaking Faith. There's more help on the way, every day.

Listen up. See what else Holy Spirit allows me to say, as I rely on Him along the way. I know you will stay tuned in. Again, I love this place I'm in — this place where everyone wins.

We can't loose with the tools God has given us to use. He has divinely equipped His saints. I thank you Lord! Continue in His blessings!

> "In conclusion, be strong in the Lord [draw your strength from Him and be empowered through your union with Him] and in the power of His [boundless] might. Put on the full armor of God [for His precepts are like the splendid armor of a heavily-armed soldier], so that you may be able to [successfully] stand up against all the schemes and the strategies and the deceits of the devil. For our struggle is not against flesh and blood [contending only with physical opponents], but against the rulers, against the powers, against the world forces of this [present] darkness, against the spiritual forces of wickedness in the heavenly (supernatural) places. Therefore, put on the complete armor of God, so that you will be able to [successfully] resist and stand your ground in the evil day [of danger],

and having done everything [that the crisis demands], to stand firm [in your place, fully prepared, immovable, victorious]. So stand firm and hold your ground, HAVING TIGHTENED THE WIDE BAND OF TRUTH (personal integrity, moral courage) AROUND YOUR WAIST and HAVING PUT ON THE BREASTPLATE OF RIGHTEOUSNESS (an upright heart), and having strapped on YOUR FEET THE GOSPEL OF PEACE IN PREPARATION [to face the enemy with firm-footed stability and the readiness produced by the good news]. Above all, lift up the [protective] shield of faith with which you can extinguish all the flaming arrows of the evil one. And take THE HELMET OF SALVATION, and the sword of the Spirit, which is the Word of God.

With all prayer and petition pray [with specific requests] at all times [on every occasion and in every season] in the Spirit, and with this in view, stay alert with all perseverance and petition [interceding in prayer] for all God's people."

**Ephesians 6:10-18 AMP**

**December 11, 2017**

Today is the day all your dreams shall come true! Believe and receive all that God has promised and released to you! In my time of sitting and listening to God this morning, this is what He spoke to me, by way of His Holy Spirit.

We will never worry about money, because He's given us the land that flows with milk and honey! Everything the devil tries to block us with, or put in our way, we will laugh at because what God has given us shall come to pass.

Remember, it's He who gives us the power to get the wealth, and we must receive our wealthy place, even in this hour. "Seed time is always harvest time for our financial further!" (Words spoken, by Apostle Leroy Thompson.)

We shall never discount, destroy or be discouraged with our seeds sown. It's God who gives us seed to sow. Planting in the right soil, we will know, because of the direction of the Holy Ghost. Planting in good soil always brings good crops. Planting in bad soil, we must stop.

"Seed time and harvest time will never cease," keep listening, believing, doing, and receiving what God has spoken to, and through me, by His Holy Spirit. Prosperity has to come when you allow His will to be done.

Victory has been won, because of God's son, our Lord and savior, Jesus Christ. In Him, we live, move, breathe, and have our total being. Why? We are spiritual beings, being led, and fed by His Spirit.

Again, obey and believe God, by following His instructions: then He will impart and cause you to grow and multiply. Believe His prophets, and receive His prosperity; that He's already released to you, by grace through faith.

> "And they rose early in the morning, and went forth into the wilderness of Tekoa: and as they went forth, Jehoshaphat stood and said, Hear me, O Judah, and ye inhabitants of Jerusalem; Believe in the Lord your God, so shall ye be established; believe his prophets, so shall ye prosper."
>
> **2 Chronicles 20:20 KJV**

I have blessed you in ways you don't know how right now. I've removed the tough off your stuff. Things that were tough to get are easy to receive right now. I'm responsible for the how. Never say why. I've allowed things in your life to multiply. This is the beginning of your great ending. The way things started out for you, will not determine where you will end up. Receive your **STUFF**:

**S**upernatural

**T**hings

**U**nlimited

**F**avor

**F**inances

These have already started coming into your house. Remember the words I spoke to Apostle Leroy Thompson: "Favor and finances, Angels are dancing around in your house. When you return home, things will never be the same.

I've blessed you in Jesus' name. There's no other name greater. This I speak will not happen later. It's happening right now. Believe and receive what My prophet has spoken out. Love like I love. This love is from heaven above. I've caused you to be harmless as a dove.

What I've given you is for all the world to see. You are showing off for Me. Receive. My glory is revealed. People will see all I've given you is for real. You can't keep still. Keep moving in My manifold, manifested miracles, and all these things shall keep coming to you. This is what I do, and have done. All because of My son! Remember this scripture I've spoken to you:

> For God so [greatly] loved and dearly prized the world, that He [even] gave His [One and] only begotten Son, so that whoever believes and trusts in Him [as Savior] shall not perish, but have eternal life.
>
> **John 3:16 AMP**

This new birth of blessings it's just to receive eternal life in Christ Jesus, you will not perish and be poor. You have received wealth and riches in your house, forever. Remember, what I've spoken again.

I am not a man. I can't lie. I've caused these blessings to multiply. Continue in My word. You are hearing and receiving words from Me that you never heard. Hear, listen, and do all that I've spoken, and continue to speak to you.

You will never be in doubt. I've strengthened you and allowed all these things to come about. It's not by your might or your power, but by My Spirit. Keep being led and you will continue to be fed. Believe and receive what I've said, and what you have read.

The words I speak are not just in your head, but in your heart. Continue to stay connected to Me, and you will continue to receive from Me, and all the world will see My wonderful works. People will see and be amazed at what I've done. Some will be saved, and others will turn and go away.

> They will say, this is the Lord's doing; It is marvelous in our eyes.
>
> **Psalm 118:23 AMP**

People will follow those who through faith and patience God has allowed to receive His promises.

> so that you will not be [spiritually] sluggish, but [will instead be] imitators of those who through faith [lean on God with absolute trust and confidence in Him and in His power] and by patient endurance [even when suffering] are [now] inheriting the promises.
>
> **Hebrews 6:12 AMP**

Finally, continue to keep My words in your heart. I will never depart. I love you from the heart. You also, must have this heart love that has come from heaven above. I am, that I am, has spoken. This is the word from the Lord!

Therefore My people shall know My Name and what it means. Therefore in that day I am the One who is speaking, 'Here I am.

**Isaiah 52:6 AMP**

## December 17, 2017

Today I woke up with God speaking to me about giving and sowing seeds in good soil.

**SIM**

**S**owing

**I**ncreases

**M**oney

**These are the Decrees God gave me:** Thank you Lord I'm a sower, I continue to give my tithes and offerings that I owe. Seed time and harvest time never cease, therefore money keeps on coming to me.

God ministers seed to me because I'm a sower, I don't have to look for money, because money always finds me. Money is attached to me, money is attacking me, and money is attracted to me. I'm a money magnet.

The wealth of the wicked is no longer laid up for me. Wealth and riches are in my house. This is why I have exceedingly, abundantly, above all that I could have asked God for.

Pastor and Lady Mary is good soil for me. KMC is where He wants this seed to be. I sow into Pastor and his wife, and all these blessings keep coming in my life. Money is needed to build up God's kingdom; therefore I continue to seek His kingdom first. All these things are continually added unto me.

Thank you God for money with Kingdom purpose. I have purposed in my heart to give. I'm a cheerful giver, and not a cheap giver. I give above what I see, and this is the faith you've given me.

I have substance of the things that I hope for, and I walk in all Your opened doors.

Thank you God for supplying all my needs, I keep on sowing my seeds. Thank you Lord for all the people that continue to sow, as they sow into people and places that they didn't know. I'm blessed indeed because of my seeds. Amen increase.

Today is another early rising. I'm up receiving and ready to release what God has spoken to me. I started with praise and worship first; it's a must. Thanking Him always. I listen to Him afterwards to see what He wants to speak next. If he doesn't speak, I begin to pray in the Spirit, once finished, then I begin to listen.

**See what He's spoken to me:** Don't let the devil distract and destroy you. Your delay is only your Divine dominion. It's already been done by grace through faith. God has already made the way of escape. Don't believe what satan puts in your face.

Faith is what you can't see right now, even when you don't know how. Increase is your birthright. You have exceedingly abundantly above all you could have ever asked God for.

Walk through the open doors. Remember the gates are opened and you drive in. You are never bound by sin. He's allowed you to come in. This is the place of regrouping, rescue, restoration, resting, and receiving all these things that been given you.

Guard your thoughts. Think things that are true, honest, just, pure, lovely, and good report. Who's report will you believe? Mine. Now receive.

> "Finally, brethren, whatsoever things are true, whatsoever things are honest, whatsoever things are just, whatsoever things are pure, whatsoever things are lovely, whatsoever things are of good report; if there be any virtue, and if there be any praise, think on these things."
>
> **Philippians 4:8 KJV**

The opposition came and went in Jesus' name. There's no other name greater. Jesus Christ didn't die and rise again in vain. The price has been paid. The way has been made. There's no need to repurchase what God has brought. You were brought with a price. Jesus paid the ultimate sacrifice. You must continue to live right.

**Listen to this song: *Lies* by Bishop William Murphy. The words of this song are key.**

This is what God encourages me, again saying, "You are free to be what God has called you to be. You are here for a reason."

The enemy tried to attack that which He gave you to come out of lack. Your seed. The seed is attacked by sowing in the wrong soil. Shopping and eating before it's time is the wrong soil. God's blessings have no strings attached.

Again you have been brought out of lack. You can never turn back. Back isn't an option. Keep believing, trusting, hearing, and listening to Him. Praying in the Spirit is a must. What satan shows and says, you can't trust.

You must keep receiving revelations and following instructions. God's will says some things that you don't understand at first. He's spoken and sent people to help in the building up of His Kingdom. Don't think it's strange when people come in your presence saying, "I've been sent by God to help." He's answered their prayer of wanting to help build up His Kingdom.

They must be taught and trained in Jesus name. They have received and responded. They only have the first part of the instructions. They are gifted, but must be lifted. Some are saved, and some desire to be saved. You are the leaders; they will understand and follow. Teach on leadership. Command, commission, and compel them to come. It's already done. Victory has been won.

> Jesus came up and said to them, "All authority (all power of absolute rule) in heaven and on earth has been given to Me. Go therefore and make disciples of all the nations

> [help the people to learn of Me, believe in Me, and obey My words], baptizing them in the name of the Father and of the Son and of the Holy Spirit, teaching them to observe everything that I have commanded you; and lo, I am with you always [remaining with you perpetually—regardless of circumstance, and on every occasion], even to the end of the age.
>
> **Matthew 28:18-20 AMP**

God's love will always overrule what satan tries to do. Keep loving Him with all your heart. He will not depart. Remember He's never far. Never go on your own. God sees and remembers the seeds sown. Keep sowing seeds that have been given to you for a purpose — Kingdom purpose, not yours. Don't ever get mixed up.

Seek the kingdom first and His righteousness, then everything else you can enjoy, what's been added unto you. Seeds keep coming. Keep sowing. Receive, what's been spoken by Me, I'm the almighty all-powerful God!

I'm up early again listening to what God has to say today.

This is a great day that He's made. I will rejoice and be glad in it. I have peace that surpasses all understanding.

> "Rejoice in the Lord always [delight, take pleasure in Him]; again I will say, rejoice! Let your gentle spirit [your graciousness, unselfishness, mercy, tolerance, and patience] be known to all people. The Lord is near. Do not be anxious or worried about anything, but in everything [every circumstance and situation] by prayer and petition with thanksgiving, continue to make your [specific] requests known to God. And the peace of God [that peace which reassures the heart, that peace] which transcends all understanding, [that peace which] stands guard over your hearts and your minds in Christ Jesus [is yours]."
>
> **Philippians 4:4-7 AMP**

As I was sitting quietly listening to Him, I saw this small bright light, as it became larger and larger. I saw this band. I saw a building with an arch shape at the front top.

I began to pray in the spirit and this is what He said: "The windows of heaven's blessings are open. God is pouring us out blessings we don't have enough room to receive, because of our obedience to give."

> "Bring all the tithes (the tenth) into the storehouse, so that there may be food in My house, and test Me now in this," says the LORD of hosts, "if I will not open for you the windows of heaven and pour out for you [so great] a blessing until there is no more room to receive it."
>
> **Malachi 3:10 AMP**

Overflow is here. Have no fear. I receive all that He's given me. The glory of the Lord is here, right now in this atmosphere.

The walls are down. Everything satan does drowns. Let the rivers flow. Flow in favor without labor. Flow in finances for all our circumstances. Flow in righteousness for all that was a mess.

You have passed many tests. Never concentrate on the test, but the testimony. Even though trials come, know that the triumph has already begun. You have won, because God has given us His son.

Supernatural money has found you. It's here to stay. God keeps on providing every day. When money gets low, we must continue to sow. Money is in your hands. This money comes with God plans — plans to prosper you, and have the expected end. You can't receive what you're not expecting. What are you believing for? Are you expecting the great to come your way?

It's okay. Decree it. Receive it. From mind time to manifestation time. What's on your mind? Begin to shine and walk in His divine all the time. God will never leave you behind.

> "For I know the thoughts that I think toward you, saith the Lord, thoughts of peace, and not of evil, to give you an expected end."
>
> **Jeremiah 29:11 KJV**

You always win. Keep the faith, trust, and believe. Again, I receive, all this money that keeps on coming to me. All because of sowing seeds. Remember the reason for the season. You have the best gift anyone could have ever given you — Jesus Christ, our Lord and Savior.

Apostle Leroy Thompson spoke, "This will be the best Christmas you ever had." It's done. Receive blessings after blessings after blessings. They just keep coming to you. Receive and thank God.

Thanksgiving always allows room for more. This is the word from God! I thank God for all He keeps on speaking to me, by way of His Holy Spirit.

The Hurricane didn't stop me; it pushed me into where God wanted me to be. I'm free. Free to receive. The time has come. You see what He's done.

Praise God, from whom all blessings flow. Worship Him in spirit and in truth. Watch Him do work in and through you.

Never give in to what the enemy shows you. Continue to pray, stay, and obey. Seed time and harvest time never cease. Money is released. More money than you ever had. Money is overflowing your bag. Extra large gifts have been released. God has spoken to the people to give to you. They have obeyed.

Now you see all this money, that has come your way — money with a mission. (Author: Apostle Leroy Thompson) This is money for the vision — money that's Ministry Minded. Money that's motivated, manifested, and moving in your direction.

You have a message; it's being delivered. You have divine destinations. Keep seeking God's kingdom first and His righteousness, and you shall continue to see all things that have been added to you. The Way-Maker, keeps making a way out of no way.

As I stared out, seeing the small bright light, it became larger and larger. God says, "This is what He's done in our lives." We took what we considered the small seeds, and sowed every day. Therefore, all these larger and larger blessings keep coming our way. Blessings that are here to stay.

Sowing money daily, brings money daily. You shall reap that which you sow. Money keeps on coming to you. (Apostle Leroy Thompson) Thank you Lord! I Receive!

Will you receive? I'm expecting to receive more. Stay tuned in and see what's in store. I'm believing as you are reading this, and you continue giving. Your money has increased, as your blessings keep coming to you. I'm believing for your salvation, healing, and deliverance.

If you aren't saved, speak this out loud, "Jesus, I believe that you are Lord and savior. I believe you died and God rose you up from the grave. God, forgive me of my sins, and come into heart, and save me now."

I Praise God for your salvation.

### See this scripture:

> That if thou shalt confess with thy mouth the Lord Jesus, and shalt believe in thine heart that God hath raised him from the dead, thou shalt be saved. For with the heart man believeth unto righteousness; and with the mouth confession is made unto salvation.
>
> For whosoever shall call upon the name of the Lord shall be saved."
>
> **Romans 10:9-10, 13 KJV**

Tuesday night at Impartation Conference, Apostle spoke: "You've been through the flood waters, and another flood is coming that will flood us with Holy Ghost power."

I just said, "I receive. Thank you Lord."

Apostle imparted the same self-anointing on me and I received. I couldn't stand because the anointing was so strong. I fell down and got back up. I feel so wonderful. I'm strengthened with God's power to do all He's called me to do. I'm so excited. I'm rejoicing, rejuvenated, resting, and receiving all that's been imparted in me. I feel like nothing can stop me. I got the power. No turning back.

While back in my hotel room, I began to pray, worship, and praise God, in the beauty of His holiness. Singing love songs to God and thanking Jesus for loving me, and asking God to keep His loving arms around me.

I'm hearing, listening, and doing. I'm experiencing Holy Ghost taking over. I love this. I say, "Keep walking with me Lord. Keep teaching me Lord." I'm flowing even in the not knowing how right now. Quickly, suddenly, this is how. Holy Ghost just answered the how, right now.

This might sound strange. However, it's in Jesus' name. I will never be the same. There's power in Jesus' name. No other name is greater.

This storm has released me into great and mighty works. People will see what's coming, not just wonder. I shall continue to speak with the power of the Word, and from Holy Ghost.

This Hurricane tried to take me out, but I never lost my shout. I gained, from this hurricane. God gets the glory in my story. Rescued, as I have recovered, restored, and I'm rejoicing — witnessing, and testifying.

This book is what is helping, even now, people deal with whatever their Hurricanes in life might be. Keep listening to me. Again, I say, the way you go through will determine the outcome. Go through knowing that the outcome has already worked in your favor. Favor without the labor. You have been brought out to be brought up to new levels and higher heights.

Keep loving God with all your might. My will is to do His will. There's flooding of Holy Ghost power, even in this very hour. I'm ready for what tomorrow will bring, in Christ Jesus I keep on receiving everything. Souls are being saved. I'm rejoicing because He's chosen me to assist in bringing them in. Enough for now. Keep tuning in, as Holy Ghost shows us how.

**Turnaround Sightseer**

It's Saturday afternoon, God reminded me of what He spoke in my book: *The Secrets Are Out:*

Turnaround and don't trust in what you see right now. Know that the unseen is being prepared for you to walk in. Don't think it's strange when they come in Jesus' name. Your life has been prophesied over, and it will never be the same.

Trust and believe my prophet because I've designed you to prosper. It has come to pass. Never worry about money again; it will continue to come in. If you knew how, you wouldn't have believed in my prophet that spoke it out, for it to come about.

I know you trust Apostle Thompson, but you want to figure out how. That's not your job but Mine. Hear Me when I speak all the time. You are walking in My divine. Every Word I've spoken has been divinely directed and delivered to you. Do what I say to do.

Put on the whole armor of God and you will go far. Follow instructions the way I've imparted them to you. This is My will. Make sure your will is to do all that I've said to do.

This has been coming for some time now. Ministry is easy. People come from me. Angels are bringing them in now. Ministering has taken place. Personal ministry of your books is being prepared, no longer will they just look. Residuals are coming in now. More money shall keep coming in.

I've given you what to write. My Word never returns void, it accomplishes what I've said, and where and who I've sent it to.

This year, and years to come, you will never fear. You have been brought from the rear. You are the leader. Never get out of place. I've placed you in this race. Keep up the pace.

Sometimes, you will run and then observe. Receive now because you have been preserved. The fire came before the pain. Holy Ghost fire will keep you in my lane.

Follow through now, you know what to do. Keep following instructions. My spirit will never lead you wrong. The pain was for my gain. You stood, as I knew you would. The pain was temporary light affliction. The turnaround has begun.

What you see now has been released to you. Now you are a sightseer. The light is on. Victory has been won, because of My son, Jesus Christ. In Him you will always move, live, breathe, and have your total being. My spirit is upon you.

## January 26, 2018, Baton Rouge, La

I've been sent to the four corners of the earth to teach and preach the gospel of Jesus Christ. I've been unchained and uncuffed to go yea therefore and spread the report.

God has commissioned me for this great mission. He's chosen me to go. Everywhere the Spirit leads me, I will follow. I have purposed in my heart to never go on my own.

I will begin to sing Jesus songs. God has brought back what I've set aside. Get back enemy, you will never ride. Under God's almighty wings I hide. I will never trust the enemy, because that would be suicide. In Christ Jesus I abide.

My God has and will always provide. My needs, He's already met. What He's done and keeps doing for me I won't forget. He's told me, "You haven't seen anything yet."

I'm His chosen and His elect: He's made me to be His very best. I'm Royal, well rounded and spiritually grounded. My roots are steep and deep.

There will be times He's talking and I can't sleep. I'm prepared to hear what God speaks to me. In the spirit, I dance and I receive His plans. I'm living heaven right here on earth. I thank God for this new birth.

I'm walking in a new beginning and this is why I'm winning. There's no losing or lacking in me. I fight the good fight of faith, and God keeps blessing me every day.

I continue to obey and do things His way. I don't worry about the negative things that people say, because God says, "Vengeance is mine, He shall repay." People can't stop me anyway. I'm rich in houses and land, because I chose to follow His plans.

God has placed this wealth in my hands. I shall continue to go yea therefore and help build up God's kingdom. This is my mission in this Great Commission. I will never lose my position.

Because I'm helping the kingdom grow, money will continue to flow, and I will always have seeds to sow. I have great reach, because I follow Holy Spirit instructions on what God wants me to teach.

Thank you God for blowing the massive souls in with the great and boisterous winds. I love this place that He's set me in.

## January 27, 2018

God does things quickly. Suddenly there was a sound of rushing mighty wind.

> And suddenly there came a sound from heaven as of a rushing mighty wind, and it filled all the house where they were sitting.
>
> **Acts 2:2 KJV**

He came quickly. Something happens in the noise. Praising God He adds souls.

praising God continually, and having favor with all the people. And the Lord kept adding to their number daily those who were being saved.

**Acts 2:47 AMP**

There's joy in the noise. Make a joyful noise. Fully recognize and know who God is. Know that we are His children. He's our maker, and we must be thankful and grateful, as we have received His manifestations. He's always faithful to all His children that enter into His gates or His presence with thankful hearts; and we go into His courts, praising Him daily with joy and gladness.

> Shout joyfully to the LORD, all the earth. Serve the LORD with gladness and delight; Come before His presence with joyful singing. Know and fully recognize with gratitude that the LORD Himself is God; It is He who has made us, not we ourselves [and we are His]. We are His people and the sheep of His pasture. Enter His gates with a song of thanksgiving And His courts with praise. Be thankful to Him, bless and praise His name. For the LORD is good; His mercy and lovingkindness are everlasting, His faithfulness [endures] to all generations.

**Psalm 100:1-5 AMP**

Shouting, the walls came down. Shout unto Him with a voice of triumph.

> So the people shouted [the battle cry], and the priests blew the trumpets. When the people heard the sound of the trumpet, they raised a great shout and the wall [of Jericho] fell down, so that the sons of Israel went up into the city, every man straight ahead [climbing over the rubble], and they overthrew the city.

**Joshua 6:20 AMP**

# Jesus is My Everything!

**January 29, 2018**

Monday after my praise and worship I began to hear these words: The blood came streaming down, there's no other love that can be found. I always want him to be around. Jesus I love you.

I will do what you want me to do. No place I want to be other than in your presence. People come and people go, where you lead me, at first, I don't even know. All I know is, I will follow.

No greater love like Jesus. You are the reason I'm here. I have no fear. Keep me near. The cross experience I know was for me.

The death burial and resurrection, I will follow in your direction. The path I take is for your sake. In Jesus' name, nothing stays the same.

Heartache can't stay. Poverty can't stay. Lack and limitations can't stay. Hatred can't stay. Depression can't stay. Prosperity has come my way. Love has come my way. Joy, unspeakable joy, full of gladness has come my way. Spiritual minded, life, and peace has come my way.

Oh, how I love to call your name. Jesus, Jesus, Jesus! When I call You, demons flee. Thank you Jesus! Greatly and greatly your name is to be praised. I worship you always. Every moment I see, taste, hear, feel, and smell, I know all is well.

*Water-Breaking Faith*

---

Everything I am, and all that I have, I worship you Jesus. All I do is in the name of Christ Jesus. He paid the price for me. If it wasn't for the blood of Jesus, I don't know where I would be. I shall forever be grateful. Thank you Jesus!

Still just amazed and thankful for all God has done, and is doing in our lives. We continue to sow seeds that have been given by God.

Money shall never depart. We keep Him in our hearts. Money continues to come, even when it looked like there was none. Money finds us.

My daughter (Tange) received a check from a job she worked at over a year ago. We had an overflow of the Impartation Conference, at the SMC2U Conference held in Baton Rouge. Apostle Thompson spoke more things in our lives and we received — awesome teaching and preaching.

What an amazing time in the Lord. In His presence I love to be. He gave His only begotten son for me. I thank God always. Everyday is a great day. This I decree and it's been happening to me. Praying in the Spirit, this is how I keep living.

The enemy will try you; therefore, you must know what to do. Speak the word, obey, and follow God's instructions. Keep loving, and keep your heart right all the time. You shall keep shining in His divine.

During these times of rainy days, I keep hoping they will soon go away. After Hurricane Harvey I don't want them to stay. That's it for now. I will talk to you more later. Remember things always get greater.

Today is another great day. God encourages me with His Word daily and I receive. I'm continuing to write what He speaks to me. I Thank Him for blessing you. Are you going to receive?

**Listen to this word today:**
God told me to expect something great to happen to me today, and He gave me this scripture. Praise God!

"So now, take your stand and see this great thing which the LORD will do before your eyes."

**1 Samuel 12:16 AMP**

**This is prophetically spoken:** The prophetic is the mind of God. Don't break your thought with God.

The year 2017 was a year of separation, severing things that you couldn't bring into 2018 (Hurricane Harvey's flood happened). God removed us out of our comfort zones, to receive on our own. We have to take what He's given us, and don't keep taking what we've been getting.

Life has been throwing us some blows — lack of money, ministries not up and running. Manifestations as God has promised. God allows you to be mad enough and sick of things and people in your life so that you can receive the right things, in this season of our life in 2018. Mega doors are opening quickly. Nothing can break this. We in the glory days.

God has also been speaking about the number Eight. On the Jewish calendar it means new life, rejuvenation, a season of the glory, and excelling. By the time the enemy finds you, you will be gone. You're moving at a fast pace.

Darkness is your G card. The glory of God shows up when His children are in what they see as darkness or devastating situations in their lives. People will see you out.

Once I received this Word from God, I began to write it down as I always do. Now, I'm excited as I'm sharing it with you. Hallelujah! To God be the glory!

As I closed my eyes, while sitting and listening for God to speak, He showed me a picture of an Octopus. I immediately asked Holy

Spirit to reveal to me what this was about. I knew it was from God, of course, but why would I be seeing an octopus?

**This is the revelation, God spoke these words first:**

1) Eight million
2) New beginning

He said, "Like the Octopus has eight legs, so do you. You have eight legs of strength."

1) Grace
2) Mercy
3) Faith
4) Righteousness
5) God's heart
6) Wisdom
7) Obedience
8) Prophetic Anointing

You have eight million to start, and many millions that are coming. Know that you have plenty money. Money is never a problem. Remember this, anytime you think you can't do, know that I've already made it happen for you. Never have any doubt that you are out.

You are out of lack and limitations, poor and poverty. You have been brought into wealth and riches now. What you thought you couldn't afford, the house is yours. I've opened the doors. Enter into My gates with thanksgiving and into My courts with praise. Always be thankful and bless My holy name: the name above every name, the name that never changes.

You have My heart. You've been given a new start. Where you began, isn't where you stand. Your position has changed. Bless His holy name. Use your eight legs of strength. You've been sent, because I've told you to repent. You obeyed. You will never go astray. Keep going My way.

The way has been made even when you couldn't see the way. Today is always your day. Your blessings are here to stay. The price has been paid. Again, you obeyed.

Unlimited books are being sold. People are doing what they were told. Your money they will not withhold. My Word is spoken through you, they are reading and receiving.

You are reaping the harvest I've promised. You know it's not just about money. Souls are coming from the north, south, east, and west. I've chosen the best. People have passed many tests. What you've decreed, you have received, know that it has all come from Me. This is the Word from almighty God! Receive.

When I close my eyes again, I see what looks like a dark door and light all around it.

You are the light in dark places. Always let your light shine for all the world to see. They will know this light you have comes from Me. My glory is revealed.

Today, I was watching the movie, *Hidden Figures* again. There were words spoken in this movie that stood out to me, like: "Every time we have a chance to get ahead, they move the finish line." I immediately began to write down those words. When God gives you a message, know that it's for the mission He's given you to carry out.

This is what God spoke to me, from those words spoken in the movie: As God's children, we must fight for what we want, and quit complaining about it. We must fight the good fight of faith, know that it's already done by grace through faith and we just have to make it manifest. We've got the power to get the wealth and whatever we want. Have the will to get it. Just like in the Prophetic

Word, He said, we have to take what He's given us, and don't keep taking what we've been getting.

In life some people leave a will to be carried out by the ones left behind. I'm not going to leave you something I think you don't want or deserve. Do you want to be saved from sins, delivered, and help others get their deliverance and live in dominion?

God so, loves us that He gave His only begotten son. That word begotten means: especially to and for us. Right here on earth, Jesus laid down his life, and died for us, so that our sins were forgiven. Then, He rose back up again, and now we can always win and not be bound in sins.

We have been given a choice, and we must choose who we're going to serve, and if we want to be saved. Jesus paid the price for us, by choosing to lay down his life. Let's follow his example. We use these Initials: WWJD (What Would Jesus Do?).

People can't take something back from you, if you already paid for it. Jesus loves us so much that He laid down his life for us. Will you love like He loves?

See this scripture:

> "By this we know [and have come to understand the depth and essence of His precious] love: that He [willingly] laid down His life for us [because He loved us]. And we ought to lay down our lives for the believers."
>
> **1 John 3:16 AMP**

Choose to give up your old life of sin so Jesus can step in, and you will win. I know, of course, no one can make you do what you don't want to, so be willing and obedient and receive the good of the land that God has in His plans.

When you've been through something devastating like Hurricane Harvey, you have to stay focused on the important purpose of our God. Never lose sight of where and what He wants you to do. We must carry out His plans always.

Again this book is a part of His purpose. We all can learn from this book, that God has me writing. I'm the first listener, hearer, and doer. Continue listening, hearing, and doing.

# The Campgound with Holy Ghost Fire!

**February 5, 2018**

Listen to this Word: What an awesome Word! Know that God loves us so. Here you go!

This is a place where the fire continues to burn, but we have to keep doing something to keep it burning. We have to keep adding wood so the fire won't go out. The wood of faith is the way. This wood of faith always allows the blessings to keep coming to us every day. The wood and faith has similarities. They both cause growth, and have substance. They both can be small or large. They both burn and build.

When we continue putting wood on the fire at the campground, it causes the fire to keep burning. The fire being large is because of more wood, which is the substance of the growth. We use the wood for building houses or other things.

> Faith is the substance of the things hoped for, and the evidence of the things not seen.
>
> **Hebrews 11:1 KJV**

When we do something, it causes us to have the outward material manifestations, or the growth of (substance) whatever we are expecting, or believing and having faith for. We then receive the evidence of what we couldn't see at first.

**Definition: Wood**
Dense growth of trees usually greater in extent than a grove and smaller than a forest.

The hard fibrous substance consisting basically of xylem that makes up the greater part of the stems, branches, and roots of trees or shrubs beneath the bark. Suitable or prepared for some use (such as burning or building)

**These two Sentence used, in the dictionary:**

1) Out of the woods.

2) Clear of danger or difficulty.

**The Most important of the two: Clear of danger or difficulty.**

**Definition: Faith**
Having the greatest belief in God for all His promises even though I have no sense realm evidence right now. I completely trust Him to always bring it to pass.

**Sentence: Having faith in God, we are clear of danger, and difficulty.**

Using both similarities because we do something, God gives us what we want, according to His will for our lives. He gave us power to get the wealth. Again, we got power and we must use it. We must continue to put the wood of faith on our fire, so it never goes out. Continue to rely on Holy Ghost fire to burn in us, through, and for us.

Keep expecting the peace, promotions, promises, and the divine dominion, and directions, to live this life of prosperity, from heaven, right here on earth — this earth that's been given to us from God, by grace through faith.

The fullness, fatness, flooding, and flowing of the milk and honey, and plenty of money, that keeps on coming to us. This campground that the devil can't intervene, invade, or interrupt the impartation, inspiration, or instructions, that are commanded from God.

This is a place that we have never been before — this place of all open doors. This place is where we all receive more. There's no little or lack. There's no turning back. The light of Holy Ghost keeps shinning in, from, and through us. This is a continual covenant connection. The fire just keeps on burning, no one can put it out, because God allowed it to come about. Shout, shout, shout!

We have made it into this place of worship, where His Word is reveal. This is a place of prophetic anointing, with apostolic authority. We decree and declare everything we want and desire, according to God's desire, we are there: and the light of His favor shines on all that we do.

> You will also decide and decree a thing, and it will be established for you; And the light [of God's favor] will shine upon your ways.
>
> **Job 22:28 AMP**

We were brought out of darkness, into His awesome light, so we must keep our lights on, and shining for all the world to see, and the manifested presence of the lord is revealed — God's Glory.

> For once you were darkness, but now you are Light in the Lord; walk as children of Light [live as those who are native-born to the Light]
>
> **Ephesians 5:8 AMP**

In this place, we are not distracted, disturbed, devastated, or destroyed by what the devil tries to bring in. We are aware, alert, and not alarmed because we understand that the weapons will be formed, but not prosper.

We know even in this place, people will talk against us, because they see our blessings. These people, we don't entertain, because in Christ Jesus we remain, and the blessings are written in our name. We know vengeance is God, He repays, and we keep doing things His way.

There is a way that seems right unto man, but it's not in His plans. Keep staying, praying, obeying, and receiving God's promises.

> No weapon that is formed against you will succeed; And every tongue that rises against you in judgment you will condemn. This [peace, righteousness, security, and triumph over opposition] is the heritage of the servants of the LORD, And this is their vindication from Me," says the LORD.
>
> **Isaiah 54:17 AMP**

> There is a way which seems right to a man and appears straight before him, But its end is the way of death.
>
> **Proverbs 14:12 AMP**

> For I know the plans and thoughts that I have for you,' says the LORD, 'plans for peace and well-being and not for disaster to give you a future and a hope.
>
> **Jeremiah 29:11 AMP**

Here it is early in the morning, about 2:30 a.m. I'm up and listening to what God wants to reveal to us. When you can't sleep, don't think it's always something wrong. Ask Holy Spirit if God wants to speak to you, and he will do just that. Let's see what God spoke. Listen in.

**Hiding Behind The Mask**

You don't have to be what you think others would like to see, just be free. Know that the son has made you free indeed.

**See this scripture:**

> If the Son therefore shall make you free, ye shall be free indeed.
>
> **John 8:36 KJV**

You don't have to hide, because God has already provided. You have healing, deliverance, wealth, freedom, right mindset, peace, protection, and promises. People are pretending to be one thing on the outside, and their insides are a mess. They are stressed, instead of choosing to be blessed.

You must decide not to hide. The devil wants you to commit suicide. Choose not to cover up, what God wants you to display. He can't just uncover you anyway. You must choose to show yourself. Look at the ten Lepers.

> When He saw them, He said to them, Go and show yourselves to the priests. And as they went, they were [miraculously] healed and made clean.
>
> **Luke 17:14 AMP**

People in sin must choose to win. We have choices in life. Choose whom you gone serve satan or our savior.

**See below:**

> If it is unacceptable in your sight to serve the LORD, choose for yourselves this day whom you will serve: whether the gods which your fathers served that were on the other side of the River, or the gods of the Amorites in

> whose land you live; but as for me and my house, we will serve the LORD.
>
> **Joshua 24:15 AMP**

When you cover things up, it could cause suffocation, suffering, suicide, and surrendering to satan. Saints have to be sanctified and soaked in the blood of Jesus. Know that Jesus died and rose again so that you don't have to suffer in sin.

You make the cross of Christ have no effect when you stay in your mess. Never be afraid to show who God made. When you are in the driver's seat, there's no defeat.

The next time you feel you want to hide, tell the devil he can't ride. Know that you pick your passenger. You control the wheel.

Now remove the mask and speak to the mountain behind it. It will move. There's always something you must do. Now you have removed the mask, the manifestations are revealed and can be received.

Manifestations are seen, and things behind the mask are unseen. Now that you have set the real person free, just be who God wants you to be. Never front or fake. In Christ Jesus you were not a mistake.

You are fearfully and wonderfully made. Know that for you, Jesus Christ He gave, and that's why He got up from the grave. All your sins He forgave.

Never hide behind the mask. You've got the power to change anything you don't like or want in your life. Follow the instructions of Holy Spirit and you will never have to hide behind the mask again. Tell satan you have shut the door.

This is an encouraging word from God. Hurricane Harvey was a beast, and we felt as through we were in defeat. We couldn't control it, but we can choose not to allow the after effects of it to control us. Following God's instructions is a must. I will constantly speak about following His lead. Spirit led and fed. Now I'm going to bed. See you next time.

Hello, or should I say good morning? I couldn't go to sleep, and I knew that God wanted to speak to me. I began to pray in the spirit, while listening to worship songs, then I began my dancing in the spirit. Oh what a glorious time in the Lord!

**After I finished worshipping, I heard these words.**
> Springing Up
> Supernatural Unlimited
> Spiritually Undeniable
> Shut Unlocked
> Speaking Unchained
> Stepped Under
> Savior Unanswered

**This is what God spoke:** This is the day of the Springing Up of Water Wells. No more drought. The waters are pouring out and overflowing. The release has taken place. People are drawing from the wells that never run dry.

> "But whosoever drinketh of the water that I shall give him shall never thirst; but the water that I shall give him shall be in him a well of water springing up into everlasting life."
> **John 4:14 KJV**

People have begun to multiply. They will come to Kingdom Minded Church with **Supernatural Unlimited** supply. Everything they've asked is **Spiritually Undeniable.** They didn't ask for themselves, but for someone else.

The doors that they opened are **Shut,** and new doors are **Unlocked.** Because of our **Speaking** Spirits, people have been

**Unchained** and released to increase. Increase in faith, Increase in the spirit, Increase in health and in wealth.

We have **Stepped Under** an open heaven. In this realm, we receive from the **Savior,** all **Unanswered** prayers. We receive now, that which was not there. Having faith in God, believing, living holy, being set apart. Our praying, and obeying, has made the way, for what we've been saying.

The glory of the Lord is here, in this atmosphere that we've created. This is where we should be and want to be. Thank God all people and things have been released. All His promises have come to me. Never lose hope, because when you are on your post, God does the most.

Great and mighty is our God, the God that's never far. He's always near, so we will never be in fear. Fear never produces fruit. Our fruit multiplies and remains because of the rain.

The waterfalls have been released to the ones that are drawing from the fountains, and standing on a solid foundation. Because of the washing and the cleansing of the blood of Jesus, we are purified. We've survived everything satan tries to put before our eyes.

> how much more will the blood of Christ, who through the eternal [Holy] Spirit willingly offered Himself unblemished [that is, without moral or spiritual imperfection as a sacrifice] to God, cleanse your conscience from dead works and lifeless observances to serve the ever living God?
>
> **Hebrews 9:14 AMP**

Now, we are released to serve in God's Kingdom without restraints. We are His restored saints. We've been reconditioned for the missions. The missions of Christ Jesus. Now, we can go yea therefore, as we've been commissioned to do.

We must continue calling, and compelling the ones that want to come. The victory has already been won, because of God's precious son. We are forever grateful for what He's done. We worship God in spirit and in truth, and keep obeying what He says do. We thank God always, and receive all these people and promises, that have been released. Amen Increase. Hallelujah!

Here I am again, ready to continue to win. Are you ready to listen in? I haven't went to bed, it's about 2 a.m. I began listening to my worship songs; I know it won't be long. God will allow Holy Spirit to speak to me in and through these songs. I pray in the spirit while listening to the songs. I've finished worshipping, and listening to God now. Ok, I'm seeing this long pavement with greenery surrounding it.

**This is the revelation from God:** God has made away, today. Never doubt, He's brought you out. The path you are traveling is straight and narrow, no room for error. Everything along side this path is green, and it grows. Nothing is dead, nor will it die. All things are made to multiply. The greenery is also for the scenery.

He leads you through the green pastures, which is this pathway. What's in between is the most important thing — the long pavement. This path has been chosen by God. Know that you will be traveling far. This path has a solid foundation, and it will soon be traveled by the nations. This is God's order.

His chosen leaders go first, to pave the way. Happy is the way; you won't go astray. These blessings are here to stay. Keep following instructions, this road has no construction. Nothing stops your view, because God is right there with you.

No signs, no wrong ways, no detours, no end of roadwork. Holy Ghost led only. There's nighttime traveling, and daytime traveling. Up ahead is oncoming traffic. Be still, and wait patiently. Your turn will come, to move on. Even though you are stopped, you won't stay or get stuck. You will come to some rest areas, however just continue to tarry. This road isn't open for all. Keep following the **GPS:**

> **G**od's
> **P**roduction
> **S**ystem

With this, you will never loose sight of the path, and the promises that have already been given by grace through faith. He's made the way.

There are things I have been given by God on this journey. I'm wrapped in the garment of praise. I'm set free to worship God in spirit, and in truth. Without the wrapping in the garment of praise, the true worshippers can't bless His Name.

My spirit is free, as God is with me. The enemy is defeated. In Christ Jesus I'm complete. It's after 5 a.m. and I'm finished with my time with God at this time. I'm always amazed, expecting, and excited to hear from Him. Now, I've been released, to get some sleep. See you next time.

God has called us to forty days of fasting and praying. Each day is a blessing, as we learn and live according to His will. We are praying forty days on KMC prayer line.

People continue to dial in to receive what God has released, through His servants. We are the ones that want to and are willing to serve Him and His people. This is a great task.

We know that God says if we are willing and obedient we eat the good of the land. We are expecting the good of the land, and the good success that He's promised us.

> "If ye be willing and obedient, ye shall eat the good of the land:"
>
> **Isaiah 1:19 KJV**

> "This book of the law shall not depart out of thy mouth; but thou shalt meditate therein day and night, that thou

mayest observe to do according to all that is written therein: for then thou shalt make thy way prosperous, and then thou shalt have good success."

**Joshua 1:8 KJV**

As we continue to travel with our Apostle Dr. Leroy Thompson, we keep sowing, not knowing which seed will bring the increase that He's promised. God keeps ministering seed to us, because He's made us His sowers. People might say or think, we need this money to repair our home. Why are we sowing like this? We understand that we can't afford not to sow. Seedtime and harvest time never cease. God has already promised the increase.

"While the earth remaineth, seedtime and harvest, and cold and heat, and summer and winter, and day and night shall not cease."

**Genesis 8:2 KJV**

We trust Him, and believe we've received. We are doing our part to cause the manifestations of the money that He's released. We also know that it's not all about money, even though the money just keeps on coming. We have peace, even after Hurricane Harvey. Are things challenging sometimes? Yes. But, we know that we are God's chosen best, set apart from the rest. We have to keep believing the money will come in, and we do what it takes according to His will to keep it coming in.

My husband keeps working, as I continue working my business, and books are being sold. Favor keeps coming. We are receiving money from places we didn't know about. To God be the glory! As our forty days of fasting and praying wind down, people are receiving what we've been praying for them. Praying for generations after generations, God has blessed the nations. Hallelujah!!!

# Prophecy of Prosperity
*End of the forty days of fasting and praying!*

**March 29, 2018**

Hello again. We have finished up these forty days of fasting and praying. Praise God! God spoke some awesome things to me. I will let you in on what He said. Here you go. See what He said.

We have received manna from heaven, and we are living under an open heaven. God lives on the inside of us. We bless Him, in Jesus' name. We have the nurturing and newness of the spirit. Encore, encore, we are more than conquerors.

Walk through the doors. God is using the remnant. We are sowers that plant seeds in the good soil, which has caused us to have good success. We have more money than we ever had before. We are spiritual beings, never affected by the disinfectant.

Things that kill others' visions, will not kill ours. Things that kill others' dreams will not affect our dreams, because we've been given many streams. God has invested, and imparted in us the information and inspiration for the up building of His Kingdom.

We have income and increase that will never cease. Money is here today, and it's here to stay, all because we continue to obey. We have power, and more power that has unfolded. This power was never hidden. This is power that we must keep using — power

*Water-Breaking Faith*

to acquire and receive what we have prayed and asked for in these forty days of fasting and praying.

Again, God has opened the doors to this place we've never been before. It's His pleasure to keep giving us more. More and more, God has opened the doors. Diamond rings, God has given us everything.

The harvest of crops has come up. You have received the money that you have been praying for. The souls have come in. Boatloads, boatloads, net breaking faith, and finances.

The white fields have been harvested. Money keeps being released, because we continue to pray without ceasing — never ending prayers and never ending money. Money that just keeps on coming.

We have reached our expected end: This end that has no ending. This end that's been bought to a specific point. These seasons of clarity of vision and God's provisions are personal growth, development, and Kingdom advancement.

The souls just keep on coming in, and we continue to win. Again, we have reached the expected end. Properties have been released, and we have the keys. Now, enter into the doors beyond the gates.

Always enter into these gates with thanksgiving: know that it's because of our giving, and we deserve and desire this way of living. Never go back, we must continue to stay on track. We were placed in the race to win, and we have endured to the end. Blessings, blessings, blessings, they have come, and will continue to come.

Victory, victory, victory, we have won. Again, we are in a place we've never been before, we see ourselves walking through the opened doors.

**March 29, 2018**

I AM

Increase

Authority

Manifestations

**Jesus The Christ**

I AM that I AM have spoken, everything that the enemy have placed on you has been broken. (Past tense) It's already done. You have been released, and restored. You shall continue to reign, now, receive. You are blessed indeed. My hands shall continue to be on you. Always keep doing what I say do. Again, I AM that I AM have spoken.

> Simon Peter replied, "You are the Christ (the Messiah, the Anointed), the Son of the living God.
>
> **Matthew 16:16 AMP**

> I know Him Myself, because I am from Him [I came from His very presence] and it was He [personally] who sent Me.
>
> **John 7:29 AMP**

God has **Increased** our going out and our coming in. We have the **Authority** to speak and get the wealth. Remember to speak what you want and not what you don't want. He has allowed the **Manifestations** to keep coming our way, they are here to stay: when we continue to pray, and obey. We are spirit led and fed.

Whatever we imagine to come, it's already done. Whatever we have seen and continue to see in the spirit realm, call it to the natural realm. I AM that I AM have released our biggest dreams. Wake up to the awesome and marvelous things. You are in My sight, when people see you living right. I AM THE WAY, THE TRUTH, AND THE LIFE. Always remember to keep loving Me with all your might.

> Jesus said to him, " I am the [only] Way [to God] and the [real] Truth and the [real] Life; no one comes to the Father but through Me.
>
> **John 14:6 AMP**

It's moving time. Receive what I've placed on your mind. Houses and land, that's in My plans. These plans that I've given to prosper you. You are at your expected end. This end that has no end.

> For I know the thoughts that I think toward you, saith the Lord, thoughts of peace, and not of evil, to give you an expected end.
>
> **Jeremiah 29:11 KJV**

The end that never ceases; the end that you have reached. The end that has no ending point. This end that I've given you what you want. Never see the end as the last thing. See the end as the destination or arrival point. This end I've called you to. This end that you have called you to: All because you continue to do what I've said, and keep saying to you.

Just like I showed you, the similarities that the rainbow has to Me. Looking at the rainbow, you can't see the beginning, or the ending, but you know it's there, because of its presence. You can't touch it or physically feel it, but you know it's there. I AM that I AM was in the beginning, even though you didn't know when the beginning actually came about, but you know I've caused you to come out: out of your mothers womb.

I ordained you before time, before time existed. Your presence here you couldn't resist. In case you didn't know, I AM that I AM and the father (God) are one.

> I and the Father are One [in essence and nature].
>
> **John 10:30 AMP**

You had no choice, because I AM that I AM chose you. Now, receive what I've given you. Right now is now. Receive in the present tense what I've given you in past tense. I give you permission to live your life out from the past, what's in this present tense.

You have reached the divine destination. You are not one of My people that just went. You are the one that I sent. You have received the revealed revelations. Know this: I AM that I AM have Increased you with Authority and Manifestations.

Now, go and bless the nations. All people will continue to call you blessed. Know this, My father will do for you, just what He heard you say.

> Now tell them this: 'As surely as I live, declares the Lord,
> I will do to you the very things I heard you say.
> **Numbers 14:28 NLT**

The blessings that's been called are the ones that keeps coming. Keep I AM that I AM residing in you, know that His people have rest: and you have been made to be His very best. Always see Me, high and lifted up. (Christ Jesus) You have been given the keys and instructions, Now, unlock and close, the doors, that He's provided the keys for.

> I will give you the keys (authority) of the kingdom of heaven; and whatever you bind [forbid, declare to be improper and unlawful] on earth will have [already] been bound in heaven, and whatever you loose [permit, declare lawful] on earth will have [already] been loosed in heaven.
> **Matthew 16:19 AMP**

Know that these are the doors that come after the gates He's allowed you to enter into. Make sure you enter into His gates with thanksgiving and into His courts with praise, as you continue to bless His Holy name. The Name above all names, The Name that will never change, and always remaining the same.

You are in charge of the blessing: the continual flow, now you know what to do. You must keep the blessings coming to you. My father has imparted, and now, increased, and given you authority to receive His manifestations. Receive now! You know how! You will never be without! Keep speaking and receiving what God allows to come out of your mouth.

# Resurrection Sunday!

**April 1, 2018**

Let us see you lifted up like never before. Let us see Jesus. I see us walking through each and every door. Everything you asked Me for is yours. All your dreams have come to you. Rest in My promises. Breathe My breath I've given you.

Allow the four winds to blow through — through the past, to the present, and into the future. Watch Me keep coming through. The whirlwind comes when I pass through. You know what to do.

Keep worshipping and praising Me like it's your last day here. Have no fear; I'm here. I Am the Great I Am. I Am your God that's never far. Keep calling on the name of Jesus. Keep Him high and lifted up. Receive your stuff, these things I've prepared, even when there was no there, and the earth was bare. Even when there, seem to be no care. Everything came because I spoke things into existence, and there wasn't any resistance.

You have My permission. Now, go and bring. Speak to the nations. You are a blessed generation. Kingdom growth and advancement has taken place. You have won the race. You kept the faith. Personal spiritual development and growth shall continue, for the purpose of My Kingdom's advancement. Never think one can work without the other.

*Water-Breaking Faith*

The two in one becomes three in one. When you walk in these two, then the three-in-one will walk with you: God the Father, God the Son, and God the Holy Spirit.

Know these are My Words I speak to you. I Am that I Am, I will never change in Jesus' name. I Am the God of all. I Am in all, and I will continue to live through all, and for all. I Am there when you call. I never will leave or forget about you, when you do what I say do.

Obedience is key, if you want to keep being with Me. Pray without ceasing. This is My way. Follow My instructions. Never depart from Me, and I will never depart from you. My Spirit lives in you, and through you.

He will keep helping you. Invitation is necessary for the reception. The price has been paid. All your sins I forgave. You got it made. Remember the keys, and don't forget or lose, them. You will not be able to enter into the doors, and you will be locked out. Don't forget to use your keys for the locking and unlocking of the doors from Me, your almighty, all-powerful God of all.

Remember to keep Me first, and you will not fall. I give you My Word! Receive now.

With what My God has spoken, it's given us a higher level in His Kingdom. We never take anyone or anything for granted. Not like we did before the Hurricane. We sometimes unknowingly might not take things or people as seriously as we should. We just believe we will be here the next day.

Well, I tell you take each day as if it's your last. Love like never before. Appreciate people, places, and things. Do and be the best you that you can be.

Within your power, trust Holy Ghost power. Obey and serve God with all your might. Love Him continually and consistently. Never deviate from the divine directions He's given you. Follow through. Never allow anything to stop you.

## Resurrection Sunday!

Worship God in spirit and in truth. Watch Him come through. He brought us out the Hurricane. We continue to rest in His Name. Yes we have found rest. This was a great test; thank God we passed. We received. Hallelujah!!!

Today I received a call from the Lutheran Church, asking if we are still in need of repairs to our home, and to see if we have returned. Of course, I'm excited now! Forty days of fasting and praying is over, and now more favor! I'm on the list to receive more favor.

Now you heard me say, they called me. There's nothing that I have to do at this time to receive this favor without the labor. Praise God! Favor keeps coming. Blessings keep coming. Favor before the finances. I'm waiting patiently, continually sowing, and expecting the great things to come, which God has already done. To God be the glory!

The drywall has been fully completed. Praise God. Seven months, wow! This is a task that takes time. Anyone out there that knows, say Amen! Anyone that doesn't, say I don't! This isn't something you would wish upon anyone, even your enemies.

Speak good and not evil. Speak life and not death, with the power of your tongue. We have won! More than before.

Moved out into more blessings. Blessings after blessings, just keeps on coming! Hallelujah!!! Shouting now!!! Always good to praise God. Listening to the singer Sinach. Worshipping with them now.

Okay, I'm back needed that praise break. Praise opens the doors that were shut. Praise shut doors that never should have been opened. Praise opens new doors that have been opened before the world began.

Just because the doors have been opened, we have to do something, which is walk in. We have walked in, and continue to walk in every opened door.

Tomorrow we believe for more favor. Every day: favor, favor, and more favor, keeps coming!

We are full of faith. What is this? Glad you asked. Lol! Answer: Having the greatest belief in God for all His promises even though I have no real evidence right now. I completely trust Him to always bring it to pass. Wow! Awesome right? I know. Lol!

We have purposed in our hearts that nothing can stop what God has started. Not even a Hurricane. In Christ Jesus we remain. We will never be the same. This one thing we know will remain. Our God will never change. I Thank Him for everything. Glory to His Holy Name!

**April 16, 2018**

Today the enemy tried to discourage me. I was as the world says, "I'm just feeling some kind of way." I didn't know what this feeling was all about, all I knew it wasn't from God. It wasn't a good feeling, so I knew who was giving. Satan. I refused to let the enemy take charge when God has given me control over everything. So I said to the enemy, "I won't except what you bring." I continued through out the day to speak these words, and kept praying in the Holy Ghost, and pleading the blood of Jesus over my thoughts.

**Here's what I spoke:**
1. Holy Ghost I permit you to go to work on my behalf and help me to obey God's will in every area of my life.
2. You are my leader and my guide, I follow your lead, help me to receive.
3. In Christ Jesus I believe, the enemy can't deceive me.
4. Help me Holy Ghost.

I kept praying in the Holy Ghost. I couldn't see anything happening yet, but throughout the day, I continued to pray. We're still believing for money to keep coming, even though it wasn't coming yet.

My daughter, Tange, told me about how she was feeling sad. She lost a close friend that she had. Her cousin was murdered. I kept saying, "Help me, Holy Ghost."

The devil was doing the most, even though I knew he was burnt toast. What do you do with it? Throw it away! I did just that. I threw the thoughts away. I canceled them. I refused to allow satan to win. Holy Ghost stepped in. I had to invite him in, so I could win. I stayed in my environment, my prayer grounds. In this place I knew that God will always be around.

The den in my home, no good news was coming in. I kept saying, "Help me, Holy Ghost."

I didn't write down any word from God today. However, He was speaking anyway. Was there a word He wanted me to hear? I kept drawing near. I kept saying, "Help me, Holy Ghost." I made it through the day with Holy Spirit's help along the way.

It's 2 o'clock am, and I still can't sleep. I listened to praise and worship songs, and kept praying in the Spirit. My husband came home from work not feeling well. Again, more bad things happening. I prayed for him, and laid hands on him. Well, I went to sleep for a few hours. Praise the lord! It's daybreak! Here's what God had to say!

**April 17, 2018**

As I go into the courts of Heaven today, this is what God revealed to me, by way of His Holy Spirit. I began to see this one story house with a long walkway going to it, and greenery all around the house. The house also had a small body of water on the sides and the back of it. This represents the path of leading us through the green pastures and besides the still waters.

> He maketh me to lie down in green pastures: he leadeth me beside the still waters.
>
> **Psalms 23:2 KJV**

The next thing I saw was a large body of water with a bridge going across and smoke all around the water. Holy Ghost revealed that this is a representation of the supernatural substance from God that shows His glory being revealed. With all this water there was a calmness and peace. The waters didn't have any waves and it weren't overflowing or flooding the house or moving fast under the bridge.

God says to us, peace be still: wait on Him to reveal. What's in store for us is for real. The enemy can't and won't be able to steal. Stay calm in the storm; it won't be long. This storm of not seeing the manifestations yet. This storm of not living in the overflow and outpouring of blessings yet. Remember I've caused the breaking of the nets. Again, it won't be long now, God decrees, if you keep following Me.

> If you obey all the decrees and commands I am giving you today, all will be well with you and your children. I am giving you these instructions so you will enjoy a long life in the land the Lord your God is giving you for all time.
>
> **Deuteronomy 4:40 NLT**

The harvest you will soon see, and know it's all from Me. Man couldn't give you what I have revealed. Your blessings have come from the field. The white fields have already harvest.

> Say not ye, There are yet four months, and then cometh harvest? behold, I say unto you, Lift up your eyes, and look on the fields; for they are white already to harvest.
>
> **John 4:35 KJV**

Plenty, plenty, and plenty of money, is coming. Because you have waited patiently, again, you will soon see. Receive from Me. Never worry about what people see and say, just know that I've caused these blessings to come and keep coming your way, and they are here to stay.

What man gives, he can take away. No one can undo what I've done. You have victory and vindication because of My son. Be happy in Christ Jesus.

Continue to live in Me. My Holy Spirit shall keep revealing and you will continue to see everything that comes from Me. Again, receive, receive and receive all these enormous blessings from Me, your almighty, all powerful God of all.

Keep obeying Me and you will never fall. Enjoy the ride. I shall always provide. My spirit is always in, with, and working through you. Remember, as long as you are in Me and I am in you, the devil does only what you let him do.

Because you had peace and calmness in the storm, you have come through with all these blessings I've promised you.

**April 21, 2018, Miami, Fla.**

Blow winds, blow. Money has been revealed, released and received by me. Money just keeps on coming to me. Everywhere I am, money has found me. I have experienced demonstrations of money finding me, because money has been dropped at my feet. I control the atmosphere. The circle is complete.

You have connected to me, even in ways you don't see. Soon you will see, my glory revealed through thee. Pray in the Holy Ghost in every space and place you are. Take charge over your surroundings.

When you pray to Me, in the name of Jesus everything is always complete. Cast out everything that I didn't allow to come about. You have the oil in your hands. Continue to follow My plans. You have come to your expected end. Prosperity is in your hands. You make it happen, and you will succeed.

> This book of the law shall not depart out of thy mouth; but thou shalt meditate therein day and night, that thou mayest observe to do according to all that is written therein: for then thou shalt make thy way prosperous, and then thou shalt have good success.
>
> **Joshua 1:8 KJV**

When you lay hands on the sick, the sick are healed immediately. What you call, comes. Only call what you want things to become. If you see lack, call abundance. If you are sick, call healing. Thank God for His will being done.

Everywhere you go, people will know that the spirit of the Lord is upon you: keep obeying what I say to do. I am the almighty God to all that will invite Me in, all who have chosen to win. My Word, continue to obey and walk in. Receive, and keep thanking Me.

Don't allow your
Pass Situations to cancel your
Present Status You have been
Promoted Supernaturally.

## April 22, 2018

**Back of ship experience**: Cruising the Atlantic, as I look across the skies I see white clouds that have a perception of blue water in between them. This is the thought that I had. I've been raised up from the bottom (blue water) to the top (white clouds) and I live under the clouds of an open heaven.

Looking down into the water, I see nice clean turquoise-looking water coming from what looks like the bottom and back of the ship. What a beautiful sight this is. Relaxing under the sun with the cool breeze of the wind. I'm thinking about how great God had created this earth, and how He's allowed us to receive of it now.

All different types of people surround us, all with the same purpose in mind — to enjoy this cruise. It's amazing what God blesses us to do. As believers, we should have this same purpose and give back to God as He's given us. Have the same purpose and build up His Kingdom. We all win and enjoy life in Christ Jesus.

Coming together for this very reason. We are in our greatest season. God has elevated us and allows us to see what's to come is far greater than what's been. Live life today and receive what's coming your way. Mediate on God's Word day and night. Everywhere we look, God's love is still around.

**April 23, 2018**

**Balcony of ship experience:** While relaxing on my balcony, I began to think as I was looking down into the waters and sailing across the Atlantic. I saw again this turquoise water coming from under the ship and the surface of royal blue waters. My thoughts were: as the ship sailed through, the water underneath separated and I saw this turquoise color, but the surface of the water was still royal blue. Without the ship sailing through the water, it stayed royal blue. Amazing right?

The ship sailing through changed the water's color and stirred up something that caused a change. I use this as an example of how we have to go through some things in order for things to change in our lives. If we stay in our comfort zones and do not allow anything to change, we will continue to be royal blue as the water's surface color was before the ship sailed through. Good or bad, we must change. I say, choose for the good, of course. God says we can choose, and of course He tells us what to choose.

We would like people to see us on the surface where we look royal blue, this is true; however, when we go through some things we look turquoise. Notice the turquoise is lighter than the royal blue. When we go through things for the good, it lightens up our loads.

The way we go through determines our outcome. You are in charge of the going through, and when God controls the one who's controlling the ship, we must know that we will make it to our destinations. Always allow Holy Ghost to help us with the sailing and going through. If the ship is rocky and tossing, hold on and take precautions, just know it's only temporary because the destinations are already planned for our success and enjoyment.

London bound; here we come. It's an awesome experience what my God has done. I hear the sound of the rushing of the waters, and I feel the great breeze of the blowing wind. I'm excited about the place He's allowed me to be in. This is a place that I choose to always win. I'm writing to let you in, and imagine as you read the place I've been. Hallelujah! Hallelujah! To my King!

This place I thank God for being in! It's a great place to be in, and I worship Him from within! Royal blue on the surface you see me praising Him, and turquoise underneath and inside, I worship Him in spirit and in truth. I make it to my destinations. What about you?

You can't physically see underneath the ship as it's sailing, just like you can't see what I do from the inside, but God does and He rewards me openly. Continue to worship inwardly and people will see your praise outwardly. Don't worry if people like it or talk about it, just know the one who matters knows and sees all. God almighty!

For those who will see me again, it's not all about sailing the Atlantic to London, but it's about the amazing things our God has done. Continue to listen in, as He allows me to let you in, into this place where we all win.

Very important day and something to keep always in my heart, so I never let these words from God depart. Read this continually. Spirit and soul lifting!

## May 6, 2018
Today God woke me up early. He spoke these words to me and I wrote them down. As He does always, He allows Holy Spirit to revealed what He speaks and I listen, and write. Thank you Lord!

# Prayer of Thanksgiving for all that God has Given!

**Let's see what He says. Listen carefully.**

Repenting Soul
Righteous Servant
Rendering Service
Receiving Supernatural

Thank you lord for all you've done for me. This is my prayer of thanksgiving. Today this is why I'm living. I have a Repenting Soul and I'm God's Righteous Servant. I'm always Rendering Service and Receiving Supernatural Blessings.

I live in the exceedingly, abundantly, always abounding in every good work and will of God. I always excel far, and there is no bar. Unlimited blessings never depart. I'm succeeding with my God on high; I'm not just getting by.

He's set me above the rest, and I've passed many tests. Because of this, I'm continually blessed. I say yes! I praise Him for He's given me His best. God's Son: It's already done. I've won.

I'm always soaring: I have strong wings and this is why I keep receiving everything. I can carry heavy loads, but I'm careful what

I hold. Burdens I have let go. Faith I behold. I can see everything unfold. Things that were told and untold.

Prophecies have been revealed. I have sealed blessings, guaranteed, granted, and they keep coming to me. Money that God has allowed, it's released, and has come to me now. Holy Spirit keeps on showing me how. I hear, listen, and do everything that's been spoken by God through him, to me.

I always receive Holy Spirit's help, and I cancel anything from anyone else. This is the way. In Christ Jesus, I stay. I won't be led astray. The blessings keep coming every day.

I'm always in expectation. I'm a blessing to the nations. Souls are saved: because of Him, I was made. In Christ Jesus, my sins He forgave. I thank God for the death, burial, and resurrection from the grave. In Christ Jesus is how I'm living. I thank God for all He's given, as I keep receiving.

This is my highest praise and I continue to bless His Holy name. Hallelujah! Hallelujah! Hallelujah! My worship and praise I give to You! God almighty and powerful God You are! You never leave or forsake me. You are always near, because of this, I will not fear. People say fear is the opposite of faith for comparison. I say, "there's no opposite; because I have chosen, what You say choose: I've chosen the blessings every day.

> Behold, today I am setting before you a blessing and a curse — the blessing, if you listen to and obey the commandments of the LORD your God, which I am commanding you today; and the curse, if you do not listen to and obey the commandments of the LORD your God, but turn aside from the way which I am commanding you today, by following (acknowledging, worshiping) other gods which you have not known. "It shall come about, when the LORD your God brings you into the land which you are entering to possess, that you shall place the blessing on Mount Gerizim and the curse on Mount Ebal. Are they not across

the Jordan, west of the road, toward the sunset, in the land of the Canaanites who live in the Arabah, opposite Gilgal, beside the oaks of Moreh? For you are about to cross the Jordan to go in to possess the land which the LORD your God is giving you, and you shall possess it and live in it, and you shall be careful to do all the statutes and the judgments which I am setting before you today.

**Deuteronomy 11:26-32 AMP**

I promise you what I promised Moses: 'Wherever you set foot, you will be on land I have given you—

> No one will be able to stand against you as long as you live. For I will be with you as I was with Moses. I will not fail you or abandon you. "Be strong and courageous, for you are the one who will lead these people to possess all the land I swore to their ancestors I would give them. Be strong and very courageous. Be careful to obey all the instructions Moses gave you. Do not deviate from them, turning either to the right or to the left. Then you will be successful in everything you do. Study this Book of Instruction continually. Meditate on it day and night so you will be sure to obey everything written in it. Only then will you prosper and succeed in all you do. This is my command—be strong and courageous! Do not be afraid or discouraged. For the Lord your God is with you wherever you go.

**Joshua 1:3, 5-9 NLT**

I thank you God for keeping me focused and in faith on these scriptures. In Christ I live, I move, and I have my total being. I live in the Spirit, I have control over the thoughts in my mind, my soul obeys my spirit, my will is to do everything according to Gods Word, and my body is healed, whole, and kept in great health, and my soul continues to prosper in all that I do. All praise and glory, I keep giving to You! My Almighty God!

## May 16, 2018

**Today our favor has been released:** The Hurricane set us back temporarily in our finances. We were in need of mortgage, our car loans were late, all bills needed to be paid, and we didn't have enough money for them all. We never wavered; we just waited on the next set of instructions from God.

He told my husband to call Dr. Leroy Thompson Jr. and he did. He gave him wisdom and a word from Apostle Leroy Thompson Sr. We followed through on the Word he gave us. He gave us scriptures, told us what to pray for, what to decree, and then sow a seed, and we did just that.

What? Sow a seed when we were in need? Yes. Seed time and harvest time never cease. This is the way to our increase. We didn't go asking for money, but wisdom on what to do. Apostle gave instructions to read **2 Chronicles 20:12, Philippians 2:13,** and **1 Thessalonians 5:24.** We did just that.

Prior to all this, I had applied to the different agencies that were giving grants for Harvey Relief. The process was moving slow, and it seemed as if the organizations with the money weren't as efficient as they should have been.

I continued to reach out to the people in charge of these funds, and their superiors. Finally, we received our approval, and the most important funds were released. Thank you Jesus!

This is definitely a faith walk. This is a long process, however we have obeyed the instructions of the prophet, and we are strong and very courageous: and know we have good success. It's already done, by grace through faith.

> "Be strong and very courageous. Be careful to obey all the instructions Moses gave you. Do not deviate from them,

turning either to the right or to the left. Then you will be successful in everything you do."

**Joshua 1:7 NLT**

"Early the next morning the army of Judah went out into the wilderness of Tekoa. On the way Jehoshaphat stopped and said, "Listen to me, all you people of Judah and Jerusalem! Believe in the Lord your God, and you will be able to stand firm. Believe in his prophets, and you will succeed.""

**2 Chronicles 20:20 NLT**

People that were in need of help has been given a hard time getting the help from those who had the funds from the grants to do so. The Houston Chronicle had been doing interviews and writing articles on people that were still in need of help, and they chose us to write about. It's nine months later, and still again, we only have drywall up.

Today we will interview with the Houston Chronicles and take pictures next week. We have been receiving help from NAM Northwest Assistant Ministries. The interview will help them get more funds to continue to help people in need of assistance. We are grateful to God for allowing them to help us.

**May 22, 2018**

**Today is my birthday.** I'm excited about having another year, twelve more months to grow in the Lord and enjoy family, friends, and build up the Kingdom of God. I'm feeling good; I'm in good health and expecting great wealth.

Although my finances are not where I want them to be at this time, I'm believing for the outpouring and overflowing of God's blessings. I'm excited about being here, while others have gone on. I'm excited to help this generation and generations to come.

I'm a sower, and God minster seed to me. I sow seeds in the soils where He wants them to be. I'm living a supernatural life, because of the soils that I have planted my seeds in, and the crops have come up. The harvest had to come. I'm speaking what I want and not what I don't want. I know God hears what I say, and gives me the very things He heard me say.

> "Now tell them this: 'As surely as I live, declares the Lord, I will do to you the very things I heard you say."
>
> **Numbers 14:28 NLT**

**June 2, 2018**

Good morning!

Yesterday was my grandson Josiah's birthday; he's one year old. I'm thankful he's here with us. The Hurricane could have taken him from us. He was just two months old at the time.

Everyday is a day to be grateful to God for every breath we take and every move we make. Some people don't have this ability, however I do. Sometimes, things come to let you know that it's God's will being done. He doesn't make bad things happen to us, however He will allow them to come. We just need to know He's always there with us.

We're His children, His righteousness ones. He's always near, have no fear. Fear comes to lock us down into the ground or grave of the how we behave. Our character is key. What's our response to the life situations that we have no control over? Human error. Someone else's mistakes. Our obedience to God's instructions, which is His Word, will save us.

**The BIBLE**
**B**asic
**I**nstructions
**B**efore
**L**eaving
**E**arth

*Prayer of Thanksgiving for all God Has Given!*

As I continually listen, and stay faithful to God, I find the finishing fortitude. I let God do what He wants to do.

**Here's what He spoke:** We see Jesus like never before, as we walk though every open door. Jesus is the way in, and we never have to be bound by sin. You will continue to win. You have a choice. Always choose life and live more abundantly.

This is where I want you to be. Receive all this prosperity; even when at the time it's not what you see. I am that I am has spoken, and He will keep speaking in you, through you, and for you, by way of His Holy Spirit. Keep inviting him in.

The power of God has risen higher in you. Keep rising to the top. The enemy isn't a match against you. You recognize him immediately and you call him out and curse him from the root: that's why he was seen at you foot. He's removed immediately, because of Me. We work together.

Since you are willing and obedient, you eat the good of the land. Since you obey and serve Me, you spend your days in prosperity and your years in pleasure. Keep allowing Me to be the love of your life. Keep Me in your heart. I will never depart. I've loved you from the start.

You are fearfully and wonderfully made, for you My son got out of the grave. I made death go away. All your sins I forgave. You are My chosen servants. I set you apart. In Christ Jesus you will go far, because there's no bar.

I'm your father and you are My child. All this prosperity pleases Me. Stay in health. You shall keep living in wealth. I am the almighty God of all who has spoken to all those who will receive Me and obey Me. Receive and enjoy! Rejoice and be exceedingly glad!

Today the money just keeps on coming. More monies have been released from places that told us no. Denied us. The denial has turned into an approval. God turns your bad into good.

Just like every time we do good, evil is always present. Because the evil is present, God teaches him a lesson, never try to stop His blessings. What the devil meant for evil, God has made it good. In the evil times we stood.

Yes, Harvey threw the line, however we still knew it was our time. We are in line; we shine and keep walking in His divine. I will never let the enemy take what's mine. My peace, my place, my position, and my prosperity: it all belongs to me. God is pleased,

> "Let them shout for joy and rejoice, who favor my vindication and want what is right for me; Let them say continually, "Let the LORD be magnified, who delights and takes pleasure in the prosperity of His servant.""
>
> **Psalm 35:27 AMP**

## June 4, 2018

Hello again! Today is another blessed day. God allows me to stay focused on Him. He takes me into the courts of Heaven to see what He wants me to see for myself and others. Each situation is different, however the same purpose of building up His Kingdom, and living a great life in it. Each day there's something I have to do, and look forward to doing it.

Some days are better than others. Challenges have come during this process, however I choose to stay in faith, and allow God to bring things my way. There were days I thought; how are we going to get through this? Again, I choose to stay focused and in faith.

**Listen to this word revealed after going into the courts of Heaven:** I see clouds all around falling from the sky and lots of people walking fast toward me. There's a long narrow never-ending path with water on both sides. White fireplace.

The glory of the Lord is here. He's in this atmosphere.

When God's glory shows up, it's like clouds falling from the sky. God's people are drawn toward the glory, to be in His presence.

Quickly, suddenly is how this should be. All things shall come to me.

Keep believing, trusting, obeying God and you will soon see. The white fireplace represents The Holy Ghost fire that's falling when the glory comes. Your time has come. Victory has been won.

Outpouring and overflowing of God's blessings has begun. You have kept the faith; everything is moving your way. The building you shall soon be in. Know that it's a blessing from within.

Worship God from the inside and receive on the outside. Within is where God resides. On the outside is where you see He has provided. Keep allowing Him to abide on the inside.

> "If you remain in Me and My words remain in you [that is, if we are vitally united and My message lives in your heart], ask whatever you wish and it will be done for you."
> **John 15:7 AMP**

You have favor. Take the step in authority and move into your blessed place — the large place that God has promised. The calls have come in, and you win. Now is the time to enter in. The gates are open; God has spoken.

You have been and continue to praise God, even when the people couldn't see. Now, enter into His gates with thanksgiving and into His courts with praise and continue to bless His Holy name. Your life will never be the same.

Don't be afraid to take the step in authority, because God has already made the way. This is the long, narrow, never-ending path with water on both sides. This the supernatural supply and surplus that He has promised to His special called out servants that are willing and obedient.

This is the good of the land, that's in His plans. Plans to prosper you and have His expected end. Never cease to serve God and His people. Never cease to seek His Kingdom first and His righteousness, and all things shall keep being added to you.

These are God's promises. Say yes, agree, and all His promises shall be. Now, receive.

**Know this:** The light switch has to be turned on in order for the darkness to go away. Light has to shine through darkness to become day. Darkness can't stay when the light is turned on or when light shines through. Light always makes the darkness go away. Whatever your dark situation is, it has become day. Joy comes in the morning. Notice it didn't say night.

## July 4, 2018

**Look at what I see!** I see green trees all around. A bench and a table. It looks like a park, a large open space.

**Listen in and see what God speaks to me!** People shall recognize the large place they are in. We are seated at the table, where we always win. This is a place of fun, growth, and no worries. Only God's elect can enter into this place. This place we have never been before. This opened place and enclosed. Where it ends isn't where it begins. We can move about freely, with no restrictions.

This place is God's great mission. We've been set in this position at the table of triumph and treasure. Faith without measure. This place we didn't pay to get in, because the price was already paid for us. This place is for God's **Righteous Servant** that's already **Receiving Supernatural.**

This place that people aren't homeless and hopeless. Homeless meaning not having a place but wanting to go to a place where there's rest and restoration. Hopeless meaning not having hope but hope being built on nothing less than Jesus Christ and his faithfulness.

We all can enter into this place, as long as we obey the One who made this place, and made it available. He is the true and living God. He's never far. He's always around, for the lost to be found. If they want to enter in, sin can't abound.

We must help those that want to come in, and show them how to get in, and win. Jesus is the way, the truth, and the life. We must love him with all our might. Enjoy and be exceedingly glad!

## No Lid

**June 14, 2018**

We have been blown out the box. We have no top. We have risen higher and higher. We have no limit levels. We have great power over devils. We have no lid to our finances, our faith, and our future. We go far beyond what our eyes sees right now. This is our Now, faith is.

> "Now faith is the assurance (title deed, confirmation) of things hoped for (divinely guaranteed), and the evidence of things not seen [the conviction of their reality—faith comprehends as fact what cannot be experienced by the physical senses]."
>
> **Hebrews 11:1 AMP**

We are living in our best years Now! Even though we don't know how right now. We live every day in our Now. We receive right now. We thank God now. Holy Spirit is leading us now. Angels are on assignment for us now. Prophecies are revealed now. Preaching have no lid now. Promises have no lid now. Promotions we have no lid now. Prayers we have no lid now. Prosperity has no lid now. Souls coming to KMC have no lid now. We have topped the bar, no lid now.

Again, we have been blown out. Out of lack and not enough, out of shortages and barely getting by. We have been moved into supernatural surplus and supply. We have multiplied. We have no lid now to our dominion, subduing, fruitfulness, replenishing, restoration, and receiving.

We are His servants, set apart, made holy, and we live in righteousness, with no lid now. Our love, our life, and our living has no limits, no lid now. We don't live to survive; we live in the supernatural, no lid now. We live in the exceedingly, abundantly, more than we could have asked God for, no lid now.

**Look at what God says here:**

> "Now to Him who is able to [carry out His purpose and] do superabundantly more than all that we dare ask or think [infinitely beyond our greatest prayers, hopes, or dreams], according to His power that is at work within us,"
>
> **Ephesians 3:20 AMP**

We have power to get the wealth and live in great health, no lid now. The sky isn't the limit because we have no limits. No lid now. Angels are bringing it all in, no lid no limits now. There's no lid, no limits, to our gratefulness and thanksgiving to God. We can never stop thanking Him, no lid now.

This is how this all came about. No lid, no limits now to our shout. We decree this all out. Our Now is never ending; we always remember God's beginning.

He's given us plenty. We can never be without any. We are one of the many. Many He's called, commanded, commissioned, and chosen, for this Great Commission.

Since He's called, we must call, and compel them to come. Since we came when He called our names, sinners must do the same. God has done the work and continues to do the work in us, as we must do the work for Him as He commanded us. We must follow Holy Spirit's lead, as we have no need. We desire, and they line up with Him, and we receive all the promises He's released, and we receive with no lid now.

Souls are saved, because of the choice we made. No limit, no lid now. Debt-free KMC. We receive the new building now, even though we don't know how. We just say wow! Look at what God has done, it's marvelous in our sights for all the world to see.

Souls are saved because of the blessings God has given. Some needed to see before they believe. God says, "It's okay, it's all from Me."

> "So the other disciples kept telling him, "We have seen the Lord!" But he said to them, "Unless I see in His hands the marks of the nails, and put my finger into the nail prints, and put my hand into His side, I will never believe.""
>
> **John 20:25 AMP**

No lid, no limits, now. God has allowed it all to come about, continue to shout, continue to speak out. Never be in doubt. You will never be without.

> You will also decide and decree a thing, and it will be established for you; And the light [of God's favor] will shine upon your ways.
>
> **Job 22:28 AMP**

**Rejoice and be exceedingly glad. This is the word from almighty God!**

It's nighttime. As I praised my God, and prayed in the Holy Spirit, I thanked God for all He's done, what He's doing now, and what He continues to do in my life. It was as if I went into a thankful mode. I couldn't stop thanking Him.

I was in a place of sweet rest: and I received all the things He wants me to possess. I'm so grateful to God for bringing my family and me out of Hurricane Harvey. He continues to bless us like never before. He's opened and keeps on opening doors.

When we see lack, He's kept us on track, because the enemy tries to attack. Only our almighty God has brought us back.

This place of praise I was in, I couldn't leave until God released me from within. My spirit and soul, I did exactly what I was told. I keep praising and knowing things have unfolded. Blessings and blessings, I behold.

I interceded for the people. I prayed their release of what was holding them and keeping them from being at peace. Kingdom building, that's how I'm living. God ordained it this way; He makes no mistakes. I accepted, and the enemy can't intercept. I won't allow satan to stop what God has started.

I'm moving on, regardless of what Hurricane Harvey moved me out of. The waters flooded my home, but not my mind. This temporary light affliction won't stop my mission. I'm not in a bad position because of my condition, although it was bad, and I was mad and sad. I've received more blessings than I ever had.

That's enough for now. I have to get my beauty rest. Good night for now, see you next time.

## June 19, 2018
### Listen up!

Overflow, overflow, overflow!

The glory of God is surrounding us, and we have received our **STUFF:**

<u>S</u>upernatural

**T**ransference
**U**ndeniable
**F**aith
**F**inances

The manifested release has begun and we have won. We win every time. We keep walking in His divine. The shine is on. Victory has been won. God has given us His son. His Pleasure is your prosperity.

Windows of heaven's blessings are opened. I see the opened windows over my head, and they are pouring out blessings and blessings, just like He said.

# Our Set Place

*See what's in store today.*

**June 19, 2018**

We are in this place that we've never been before. I see us walking through every open door. We are in this place; God's got us in. We are in this place without any sin. We are in this place that we always win. We are in this place that we obey Holy Spirit over and over again.

We are in this place that we remain in Him, in Christ Jesus we live, we move, and we breathe. We are in this place we always receive. We are in this place where we are never deceived. We are in this place even before we were conceived. We are in this place where we want to be. We are in this place where God almighty is pleased. We are in this place of prosperity.

**June 23, 2018**

It's night now. Everyday is a great day to be alive. I praise God for what's He's done. Hubbie and I had a great day, all throughout the day. The Hurricane didn't take our joy away. I prayed for the people. I spoke blessings after blessings for the people, my family, friends, and myself.

It's praise and worship time now. As I listen to my praise songs, I worship God in spirit and in truth. This is what I choose to do. He gets the glory!

I dance because of who God is. I dance because He's given me this praise. He's called my name. I will never be the same. All things have changed. My heart is filled; my soul is blessed. The people have been delivered out of their mess.

Souls are coming into the kingdom like never before. God has opened all the doors. This is like something I've never seen before.

I'm seeing things in the spirit now. Listen and you will see from what you hear. Have no fear. God is near; never far. He's pouring out blessings. Overflow.

So many people are coming into the kingdom — the lost, sick, hurting, and confused. They are healed, delivered, and found; no longer bound. What an awesome God!

As I continue to stay tuned in. I hear the sound. It's reigning. People have been released and restored back to their original position. In the beginning, we have been given dominion. We are subduing, replenishing, and multiplying. Increase and abundance is always our supernatural supply. We still have what God has given.

Somehow, we may have taken a wrong turn, but we have repented and returned, back to the beginning where we first received, and continue to receive. Thank you Lord!

As we keep living in the light, because we are children of the light. Darkness cannot overrule our light. We are shinning, and all the world sees. We see Jesus, therefore people see Jesus through us.

Holy spirit keep feeding and leading us. This is a beautiful place to be. Through our partnership with the Holy Spirit, we can never loose. We always choose him.

We hear, listen, and do. Obedience is key. He allows all these blessings to keep coming. Souls saved, supernatural surplus, and spiritually sound. God is always around, never far, always in our hearts. Praise our almighty God! Thank you Lord!

After I finished praying in the spirit again, this is what God speaks:

Roses are covering the gardens that He allows to grow. Our houses are blessed from the overflow. Kingdom of God is blessed because of our tests that became testimonies.

Once we entered in, we helped others get released from sin. Pick up the roses. Smell the roses. Look at their colors. There are different types of colors, just as there are different diversities of gifts, however all for the same purpose — all to serve the one and only true and living God, Lord of all. Who will receive Him?

Cover the garden and they continue to grow, as the blood covered us, even when we didn't know. Now we have Jesus, who showed us the way in, and we have been released from sin, and we always win again and again. We are covered. We can't loose, with the tools we have been given to use.

**See this scripture:**

> "In conclusion, be strong in the Lord [draw your strength from Him and be empowered through your union with Him] and in the power of His [boundless] might. Put on the full armor of God [for His precepts are like the splendid armor of a heavily-armed soldier], so that you may be able to [successfully] stand up against all the schemes and the strategies and the deceits of the devil. For our struggle is not against flesh and blood [contending only with physical opponents], but against the rulers, against the powers, against the world forces of this [present] darkness, against the spiritual forces of wickedness in the heavenly (supernatural) places. Therefore, put on the complete armor of God, so that you will be able to [successfully] resist and stand your ground in the evil day [of danger], and having done everything [that the crisis demands], to stand firm [in your place, fully prepared, immovable, victorious]. So

stand firm and hold your ground, HAVING TIGHTENED THE WIDE BAND OF TRUTH (personal integrity, moral courage) AROUND YOUR WAIST and HAVING PUT ON THE BREASTPLATE OF RIGHTEOUSNESS (an upright heart), and having strapped on YOUR FEET THE GOSPEL OF PEACE IN PREPARATION [to face the enemy with firm-footed stability and the readiness produced by the good news]. Above all, lift up the [protective] shield of faith with which you can extinguish all the flaming arrows of the evil one. And take THE HELMET OF SALVATION, and the sword of the Spirit, which is the Word of God. With all prayer and petition pray [with specific requests] at all times [on every occasion and in every season] in the Spirit, and with this in view, stay alert with all perseverance and petition [interceding in prayer] for all God's people."

**Ephesians 6:10-18 AMP**

Receive this word today and keep praying in the spirit. Watch God make it all happen for you. Make sure you follow the instructions He's given you. Don't deviate, keep straight, He makes no mistakes. Until next time, stay the course, I will return soon, with more great news. Good night for now.

**June 25, 2018**

This week is a week of praise. I bless God's Holy name. The name above every name, His name never changes. In His name I will not remain the same. Everything works for my good. In His name, I might be misunderstood. Through it all, I'm all good. Favor after favor continues to come to us. People are helping us to rebuild our home. They came from near and far. We are truly blessed. The people are excited to help, and we are very grateful. We celebrated afterwards with the workers and volunteers. We say cheers!

## June 26, 2018
Today God spoke these words to me:

1. Posture in our Praise
2. Peace for the People
3. Promises of the Prosperity
4. Put it in this Position
5. Power in this Place

This is the revelation from what He spoke: We have **Posture in our Praise** as we bless His Holy name. The name above every name. God's unchanging name. God has given **Peace for the People.** We receive this peace now.

**Promises of Prosperity** have been released, it will never cease, because He's given it all to me. I'm forever grateful, now I have received, and I can bless the nation. Now His people are blessed generations after generations. This is His commission for our great mission. Thank God He **Put us in this Position.**

There's **Power in this Place.** We have been called to this race. We are here for Jesus sake. We are not concerned about how fast we run. We thank God the race has begun, because of His son.

Victory after victory, we have won. We know there's a finish line, and we complete the race every time. We win every time, because of our endurance until the end. Just because you didn't make it to the finish line first, doesn't mean you didn't win, you won when you entered the race.

Obedience is key, and instructions are always to be followed. Preparation is a must, for the just — practicing and learning His precepts. Glorifying God by being willing and obedient to His **Precepts, Principles**, and **Practices:** this brings **Provisions, Promotions, Promises,** and **Prosperity** to His **People,** and builds up His Kingdom.

This is the proof and acknowledgement of our agreement with the ministry, and the work of the Gospel and the Church. Gospel is free but it takes money to carry it out.

**What you agree with is what you have.**

> Make me understand the way of Your precepts, So that I will meditate (focus my thoughts) on Your wonderful works."
>
> **Psalm 119:27 AMP**

# *Listen in!*

**June 28, 2018**

Let the praise begin. Thank God for the place we are in. Overflow after overflow, KMC is where people go. Growth and development is a must. People have been brought out the dust and dirt. They have no more hurt. The dust was little, but the dirt was a burying burden. All barriers are broken. God has spoken. Never return to the place you've been delivered from. This place is a place of no return. However it was God who brought you out. Shout. Praise is how this came about. Praise on the outside, releases worship on the inside. Worship from within.

**July 16, 2018**

Today was a great day. I took time to rest. After a week of Camp Meeting, we came back refreshed, refueled, renewed, and ready to continue reaching the people. Believing the lost will be found, and the faithful will be fulfilled, and carry out His will. His will and our will connected in agreement, and in alignment. This causes us to have access to His promises; which has already been given to us by grace through faith. In my resting time, God keeps speaking, by way of His Holy Spirit. Here's what He had to say.

1. Rest on His Promises
2. Reflect on His Precepts

3. Recognize His Provisions
4. Remember His Practices
5. Remain in His Plans
6. Revive His People
7. Receive His Prosperity

These seven things, is awesome news. I'm excited to share it with you.

God gave me this great news, and on yesterday I received hurtful news. A Pastor we loved went home to be with the lord. This was very shocking, because we fellowshipped with him in Camp Meeting.

When you hear of this, it makes one grateful to still be here, and to have your loved one with you. Never take life for granted, always be grateful. Love, appreciate, and be thankful for life, and the people that you spend life with. Don't neglect time. Time is vital, never to be wasted.

**July 17, 2018**

**Listen to this today!** Today is a great day. I expect something great to happen to me today. In my early rising, I'm hearing and listening again. It's so important to hear, listen, and do, what God speaks to you. Holy Ghost is key to all things happening to me.

As I reflect, remember, and recall, I know Jesus paid it all. I'm designed never to fall. I stand tall. I never drop the ball. God's blessings continue. I'm blessed through it all.

All things have worked together for my good: because I love God, and I'm called according to His purpose. I follow His purpose, which is to compel, and call people into His Kingdom. His Great Commission. I purpose in my heart to give. This is how I live. Giving is another key: for all these blessings to keep coming to me. Yes! Today it's personal.

When you obey Holy Spirit in your giving, and the money is short; know that the blessing is, all checks were paid. You never listen to what the enemy say. He puts the thought in your mind that it's not supposed to happen this way. How do you know that? Every test will turn into a testimony. You are just charting your course to help show others the way. Make your trail. Know that in Christ Jesus, we never fail. God has allowed His angels to deliver our mail. Go check it.

Believe what you see. Money just keeps on coming to me. This is what I continue to speak. He keeps providing for the Kingdom. He keeps giving seed to the sower, and His Holy Spirit tells you which soil will produce the supernatural harvest.

Continue to purpose in your heart in giving, and continue in this blessed living. People will see these marvelous things that the Lord has done, all because of His son. Know that the victory has already been won.

**Remember this Key Note again: Satan lost his mortgage on your house. It's been paid for by the cross of Christ.**

Live obeying the mission. Stay in position, regardless of the opposition. Know that Hurricane Harvey came only to reposition. You have been brought out from the storm: and released from the norm. You came out without the smell of smoke, because of what God spoke.

Know that you receive, because of what you speak. In the beginning there was darkness and no form. God spoke all things so that they exist, just like He made you, and you couldn't resist. The world had to be here, and so did you.

Remember, you were ordained before you entered your mother's womb, just like Jesus had to be risen from the tomb. Remember all these things that had to happen, and they did.

God keeps giving you revelations of the things that were hidden. All these things keep coming, as I continue to pray in the Spirit.

Holy Ghost revealed revelations, as I keep speaking to the nations. God's word will continue to be spoken to generation after generation, and people will keep being blessed throughout the nations.

Now, refuse to lose all that's been given to you. It's already done, by His amazing grace, through faith. Keep believing, having faith, and expecting the great. You are a blessing always, and are going great places and making things happen. Taking it by force! Rejoice! Hallelujah! Hallelujah! Hallelujah!

Keep trusting, obeying, and relying on God to make it happen. This is what God spoke, to you and to me. I took it personally, so can you. Remember: hear, listen, and do.

My situation was the Hurricane. What's your situation? Know that as He did for me, you can receive the same, in Jesus' name. God has spoken. The barrier blockers are broken. Don't be tempted because of the tests. God has given you His best, and you will excel far greater than the rest.

Never receive what satan suggests. If you join in with satan and his mess, you won't receive what God has allowed to manifest.

## July 19, 2018

**God woke me up with this word:** God has brought us into a land that flows with milk and honey and plenty of money. A land of brooks hills fountains. He has removed all mountains. Marinate and mediate on God's Word daily. **Respect Him** by following His instructions, and **Expect Him** to bring it all to pass.

> "If the LORD delights in us, then He will bring us into this land and give it to us, a land which flows with milk and honey."
>
> **Numbers 14:8 AMP**

"For the LORD your God is bringing you into a good land, a land of brooks of water, of fountains and springs, flowing forth in valleys and hills; a land of wheat and barley, and vines and fig trees and pomegranates, a land of olive oil and honey; a land where you will eat bread without shortage, in which you will lack nothing; a land whose stones are iron, and out of whose hills you can dig copper. When you have eaten and are satisfied, then you shall bless the LORD your God for the good land which He has given you."

**Deuteronomy 8:7-10 AMP**

"But his delight is in the law of the LORD, And on His law [His precepts and teachings] he [habitually] meditates day and night. And he will be like a tree firmly planted [and fed] by streams of water, Which yields its fruit in its season; Its leaf does not wither; And in whatever he does, he prospers [and comes to maturity]."

**Psalm 1:2-3 AMP**

"Whoever despises the word and counsel [of God] brings destruction upon himself, But he who [reverently] fears and respects the commandment [of God] will be rewarded."

**Proverbs 13:13 AMP**

### July 31, 2018

**This Year**: We will receive from God like never before. Everything in our lives will explode. Expect, watch, Thank Him, and receive things as they unfold. Don't wonder if, or question is this God? Don't say how? Just receive Now. God has given us a voice to be heard, all across this world. Things will happen quickly, before your eyes. Everything will begin to multiply. Increase and abundance is your supernatural supply. Keep loving God and His people. You will have a **WOW** experience.

<u>W</u>ind
<u>O</u>f
<u>W</u>ealth

The blowing of the Boisterous Wind, has begun to blow the blessings in. This wind can't be stopped. Just like the Hurricane when it has picked up power from its source and can't be stopped, God is the source, with all power. He's sent the Blowing Boisterous Wind of Blessings that can't be stopped.

People will see this wonderful work that God has done: all because you trusted Him when there was none — even when your bank accounts were almost empty, down to the last few dollars. He knew that this was a tough pill to swallow. You didn't stop. You continued to follow. Because you didn't stop, and you trusted Him with your last few dollars, He won't stop the wind. You will always win.

Trusting God and having faith is always the way. You continued to hear what God has to say, and you obeyed. You continued giving, even when the enemy tried to give his opinion. You chose to keep listening and hearing God's Word, reading His Word, mediating on His Word, and putting your faith into action. You know that faith without works is dead. This is why you continued to be fed, and Holy Spirit led.

> "Just as the body is dead without breath, so also faith is dead without good works."
>
> **James 2:26 NLT**

Whatever situation you are facing, you must see what God has to say, and then do what He has already spoken and keeps speaking to you. Listen and adhere to what God's prophets speak. Great things shall happen for you, even in this week.

Respect God and expect Him to move in every situation. You must obey without any frustration or hesitation. Have no fear. He is here, always in the atmosphere.

Wherever you go that's where God is. He never leaves or forsake you, when you continue to do what He says to do. You have been put in places before the nations. Because you are in Christ Jesus and he's in you,

God is everywhere you are. He's never far. Again, God says, "Your giving and living has topped the bar. You have no limits. No containment. No traps. No tricks. Just trusting. Triumphing." Notice the "ing" at the end of each of these words, this means everything God speaks in a continuation.

"Remember I have set you before the nations. People will hear what I have to say through you. It's never too late when you do things My way. Quickly, suddenly, you shall see the manifestations have already begun, it's done."

Victory has already been won. Always continue to live in My Son, Christ Jesus. Hear, listen, and do, all that God keeps saying to you. This is the Word from your almighty, all-powerful God! Enjoy!

This is the powerful word God spoke to me this morning, just as I woke up and began to listen. I didn't say a word or pray. I just listened. Sometimes, He wants you to just be quiet in the still moments of the morning, or whenever your moments are. You will just begin to see things flash across your eyes, or hear what He's speaking. You must just listen and let Him speak. You must know that it's God.

Once He starts speaking, I start writing. I never want to miss out on this precious moment with Him. This is such an awesome presence. Early mornings, like His Word says, "When they rose early."

> Early the next morning the army of Judah went out into the wilderness of Tekoa. On the way Jehoshaphat stopped and said, Listen to me, all you people of Judah and Jerusa-

> lem! Believe in the Lord your God, and you will be able to stand firm. Believe in his prophets, and you will succeed.
>
> **2 Chronicles 20:20 NLT**

This is my time to enjoy the divine presence of My God. It's wonderful. There are no worries. I continued to listen as I was writing. I always stay tuned in to hear without fear, knowing my God is always near. He has my ear. What about you?

I hope this blesses you, as it always blesses me to hear from my awesome God. Take those still moments and hear what He has to say. Respect and expect God to always bring great things your way, every day. Make it a great day of expectation. Receive His blessings!

> "So now, take your stand and see this great thing which the LORD will do before your eyes."
>
> **1 Samuel 12:16AMP**

## August 4, 2018

Good morning all. I trust today will be a great day. These two days have been awesome. Waiting at the Columbus Airport, God is speaking. What an awesome God He is. When He speaks, remember always: hear, listen, and do.

Listening to praise and worship songs along with praying in the Spirit, I begin to listen, as I know how to do; hopefully you do to.

I'm looking outside the window, waiting to board my flight and God began to say, "Today is the day that great things have come your way."

In this early morning, as we praise God, He released things that we had been believing in our hearts.

Just as the lights surround the runway and the planes sit, that's how God's angels surround us. They are encamped all around and about us. The lights bring the thing that allows us to see, and the planes take us where we are going. Without the things that are necessary, we can't get to our destinations.

God has prepared us with all these things beforehand. He's given us His plans. Plans that we shall prosper and have good success. We don't have to worry and wonder if we are blessed. Just being here to see all that surrounds us is a reason to know we are blessed. Thank you Lord!

I was thinking just how blessed we are. Some great people, family and friends are with Him now, however we are left here to finish the work He's called us to do. We are blessed going out and coming in. We live in the overflow, you know! Thank you Lord!

Again, I say it's not just about stuff, but standing — standing strong in the power of His might. As daybreak comes, and continues to come, know that it's God's will being done. We are His obedient servants, ready to serve, and happy to serve. What a blessing!

I love learning these lessons! Holy Spirit is my teacher. Again God says, "Obedience is the key, to continue following Me!"

Boarded the plane with favor already — we have been upgraded to First Class! Praise God!

Looking forward to seeing what's in store at home. Enjoy today. Choose to make it great, regardless of what comes your way.

# God told me I was His MC

## Master Caller

**August 7, 2018**

What I command will come, because it's His will that has been done. Everything I command, I must say, "Because I'm a Master Caller, and I have commanded, and called, it's according to God's will and it's already done. I believe, I've received, and I thank God for it. In Jesus name, it's done. Angels bring it to me now."

Before I went into the courts of Heaven, I commanded certain things to come, and Holy Spirit instructed me to say what God spoke to me beforehand. "I'm His **MC** — **M**aster **C**aller."

**This is what I saw after I entered into the courts of heaven:** Chains wrapped around people. Chainsaw. Brick building with large square glass windows surrounding it.

We have the tools to remove everything that has held us down. Release yourselves now. The church building is ours now. We didn't have to go far, it was always near. We had to get in a place to hear. You have heard from Me. Take the step now. Go and tell them, the Lord sent me here. They will know what to do next. It's already done, because it's in My will. KMC has been filled. This is the Word from God.

Next, I commanded deliverance, and living in health for myself and the people. I commanded increase, multiplication, and abundance. I decreed this before, however I wasn't a Master Caller at that time, and God hadn't revealed to me through Apostle Leroy Thompson that I was a Wealth Commander and that I'm to start commanding things to come. God also revealed I was to command the angels to bring it all to me after I've commanded things to come.

**These words were spoken to me:**
Levels
Launch
Love
Live
Life
Succeeded
Soaked
Supernatural
Superb
Sustained
Substance
Supreme

I've been promoted to higher **Levels. Launch** out with God's **Love. Live Life** according to what He's promised and positioned me to receive, which is His plan that has been given to prosper me, and I've **Succeeded.** I receive. Thank you Lord!

I have succeeded and gone far above the rest, because He made me. I'm His very best. I'm **Soaked** in the **Supernatural**, a **Superb, Sustained Substance** of the **Supreme** God of all god's. I respect and expect Him to always move on my behalf, and for others that I intercede for, on their behalf.

I will always obey and do what He says. He has given me and will continue to do for me the very things He hears, and has heard me say. Every approval I've been waiting on has been granted. My credit score has increased to the maximum, because this is what the world system requires.

God has showed the world, He's given His people what they desire. Nothing will stop us. God says, "Go ahead world system, inquire." Check the report, and see the marvelous thing that's He's done.

Victory has been won, because of His son, Christ Jesus. We have received because of this very reason. We have already received, and must continue to receive in every season.

We live in miracles signs and wonders. Allow the gifts to flow, even when you don't know. Holy Spirit reveals, as God allows you to be the show. People will see the marvelous things that God has done. He will keep allowing these things to come. He repeated it again in His Word, and we shall continue to repeat and command what He's said. Keep believing, receiving, and thanking God for it all.

See scriptures below:

> "When these signs come to you, do for yourself whatever the situation requires, for God is with you."
>
> **1 Samuel 10:7 AMP**

> "These signs will accompany those who have believed: in My name they will cast out demons, they will speak in new tongues;"
>
> **Mark 16:17 AMP**

> "I assure you and most solemnly say to you, this generation [the people living when these signs and events begin] will not pass away until all these things take place."
>
> **Matthew 24:34 AMP**

"I assure you and most solemnly say to you, this generation [the people living when these signs and events begin] will not pass away until all these things take place."

**Mark 13:30 AMP**

"who came to Jesus at night and said to Him, "Rabbi (Teacher), we know [without any doubt] that You have come from God as a teacher; for no one can do these signs [these wonders, these attesting miracles] that You do unless God is with him.""

**John 3:2 AMP**

**August 14, 2018**

I'm up late. This is what I'm doing and receiving. Praising and worshipping God. Praying in the spirit and listening is key. **Here's what God spoke to me:**

Download
Detach
Distractions
Disappear
Delivered
Detour
Divine
Directions
Destinations
Dominion
Drained

We must **Download** the word of God, and **Detach** ourselves from all the **Distractions.** Make the enemy **Disappear** from our thoughts that God has **Delivered** us from. We won't **Detour** from the **Divine Directions** that have been set up for the **Destinations** which cause us to have **Dominion** in our lives. This was set up in the beginning.

Never be **Drained** by things that won't remain if we just call on Jesus' name. Nothing can stay the same; things must change, including things that held us down for years and things that brought us tears and fear. Things we must not continue to hear. Remove and replace the things that kept us out of the race, and caused us to lose our place.

This place that was set here before time. The place God spoke of and allowed us to shine. The light that's brighter than all lights. We are made in the image of this light — Christ Jesus.

Remain in remembrance of the reason for every season. Every day is another day to give Him glory. Thanksgiving, praise, and worship are always in our spirits, as we worship Him in spirit and in truth.

Listen closely to the sound of the heart beating. The beat goes on. The rhythm is key. Stay in line with Me. When the beat fades out, nothing can come about. No life, and no sound can be found.

Lift God up, as you receive more than enough. New life has begun; take a run. Now we are set back in this race, for Christ's sake. Focus and finish. We always win when we get in.

Completion is a must. Stopping isn't trust. Keep pressing forward and pushing with power, if we want to be pleasing.

God's will is for us to succeed. He's already met the needs. Exceedingly and great rewards for those that stay on one accord. Together we all win, if we are without sin.

Never give your place to the enemy. Never help him destroy you. Stay in obedience by doing what God says to do. Enjoy the prize! Higher calling in Christ Jesus! This is why we receive season after season! Continual blessings for God's very elect!

I Thank God for this day — the day of approvals. God said they were coming, and they are here. The denials were tuned into approvals. No one can stop what He's started. Praise God!

Now we can get ready for the floors to be repaired, and continue the rebuilding process for our house. We are ready to set appointments. Thank you Lord!

Stay tuned for updates. It's sleep time now. It's 4 a.m. Now that I've listened in and received, it's time for me to sleep. See you next time.

**August 17, 2018**

Today is a great day! More money released, and help to complete. Complete the rebuilding of our home, just like God promised He would do. We were out of town, and money came. In Plainview, Texas we were being imparted at the SMC2U Conference, Apostle Thompson.

While we were praising God, He was releasing money. While we were sowing, money was coming. What an awesome conference. When we were experiencing lack and little, God released more than enough. Money just keeps on coming. (Apostle Thompson)

Again, obedience is key, to keep the money coming to me. I decreed that God make me a sower, and I will keep sowing: therefore the seeds keep coming. I have purpose in my heart to give, this is how I live. We needed money and help building back up, and God already knows what He's going to do: He's allowing money and help to come through. Hallelujah!!! Praise God! Thank God!

**August 21, 2018**

Good morning! This is the second day of prayer on Facebook live. **On August 7, 2018,** God called me to be His

MC — **M**aster **C**aller.

He's commissioned me to pray for the people daily at 6am.

### IHOP

**I**mpartation

**H**our

**O**f

**P**ower

Praise Him! After I finished up praying, God allowed me to continue praising and praying in the spirit.

**This is what He told me:** God is faithful! He's allowed people to hear Him like never before. He's opened every door. We must know how to walk in, as well as enter in. The way we go in will determine if we stay in.

Enter in with thanksgiving, and with praise. Bless His Holy name. Don't go in with the wrong mindset, because you haven't received everything yet.

Don't hinder your help. Holy Spirit is the help you've been asking for. You must be Spirit led and Spirit fed. Keep those wrong thoughts out of your head.

Let this mind be in you, which was also in Christ Jesus. He's the reason for the doors that have been opened. Be grateful.

You have more than ever before. You have planted, it's been watered, and now God has given the increase. In your going out and coming in, be thankful over and over again. Never look down on people or things that brought you through. Be thankful and know God brought you out and gave you these things. Praise God! Thank you Lord! I receive!

Have an awesome day. Respect God and expect His greatness. Enjoy!

**August 22, 2018**

Good morning! Today is another great day that the Lord has made, I choose to rejoice and be glad in it. I expect something great to happen to me and my family today.

I'm sharing with you how I'm making it through this after effects of horrible Hurricane Harvey. Only God is keeping me. Glory Hallelujah! Praise God! Thank you Lord!

Yesterday we received a denial from someone that already gave us an approval. The devil is a liar. I'm expecting that denial to turn back into an approval. What I call comes. I remember what God already said and has done. Victory I have won, because of His son. I call and keep calling on the name of Jesus. The adversary can't resist what I say.

I see the windows over my head: and they are pouring out blessings, and blessings, and blessings. They are doing just what God has said. Yes God causes windows to talk. He can do anything for those that please Him.

Prosperity is here, have no fear. God is near. He's never far. Our blessings have topped the bar — unlimited lifetime blessings. Receive them now. God has allowed them to come about.

Because of your obedience, you are praying without ceasing. Discipline has begun. Because you trust and continue to receive training, you have won. Because you didn't despise the small beginning, I have given you great endings.

Your now is always activated by your next. Right now blessings are always causing your next manifestations to come. Your love language will never stop. Keep the love flowing.

Your voice shall continue to be heard, because I gave you the voice. You are my mouthpiece; keep serving Me. Watch Me show people who I called you to be. What I allow you to show will cause people to grow.

In Christ Jesus is where you succeed. Continue to follow Holy Spirit's lead. I will feed you until there is no more.

Continue to walk in My opened doors. Your steps are ordered and your stops are the unlimited overflow. Stay in obedience and receive the outcome of the outpouring. Exceedingly abundantly, above all you could have imagined or asked Me for.

Massive numbers of people are coming to the Kingdom because of your voice. I made and chose you, and it wasn't your choice. Now, you are my show. Your boisterous bountiful blessings will cause the people to believe in Me.

This is My order, know that you are not out of order. You are in line, and have been made to shine in My divine. It's your time. Continue to walk in it, this place of every opened door.

Come into the gates I've opened, always with thanksgiving. Know that this is how you shall keep living. No one can take or make it any other way. You have been brought into the good land, brooks full of water, fountains and springs are flowing in the valleys and hills I allowed you to come through.

> For the LORD your God is bringing you into a good land, a land of brooks of water, of fountains and springs, flowing forth in valleys and hills; "a land of wheat and barley, and vines and fig trees and pomegranates, a land of olive oil and honey; a land where you will eat bread without shortage, in which you will lack nothing; a land whose stones are iron, and out of whose hills you can dig copper. When you have eaten and are satisfied, then you shall bless the LORD your God for the good land which He has given you. "Beware that you do not forget the LORD your God by failing to keep His commandments and His judgments (precepts) and His statutes which I am commanding you today;
>
> **Deuteronomy 8:8-11 AMP**

# The Great Commission

Keep blessing Me, by blessing My people. Keep the **TRUST:**

> <u>T</u>each
> 
> <u>R</u>each
> 
> <u>U</u>nder
> 
> <u>S</u>tones
> 
> <u>T</u>renches

Jesus came up and said to them, "All authority (all power of absolute rule) in heaven and on earth has been given to Me. Go therefore and make disciples of all the nations [help the people to learn of Me, believe in Me, and obey My words], baptizing them in the name of the Father and of the Son and of the Holy Spirit, teaching them to observe everything that I have commanded you; and lo, I am with you always [remaining with you perpetually--regardless of circumstance, and on every occasion], even to the end of the age.

**Matthew 28:18-20 AMP**

When you obey and <u>teach</u>, you will have rescued and <u>reached</u> the people that were <u>under stones</u> and <u>trenches</u> — My Great Commission.

**August 24, 2018**

On the plane headed to Atlanta Georgia, to hear Apostle IV Hilliard. It's been a while since we have been in his presence. Something powerful will happen tonight. We are ready to receive.

**See what God spoke to me:** The Holy Ghost's fire has burned off everything that's been holding you down. You are released to receive from Me. I am the almighty God that has spoken. The enemy's power has been broken.

Supernatural and beyond breakthrough, I've made it all happen for you. Keep doing what I've called you to do. I'm pleased with you. Whatever you have asked and shall ask Me, I will do.

You have succeeded far above the rest. You are My very best. You have passed many tests. I've seen your faithfulness. Keep moving by My Spirit. Watch Me keep opening up windows from heaven and continue pouring out blessings for you — flowing, and flooding in your finances. This is how fast things will happen for you.

Keep praising and praying. Never stop the work I've called you to do. Continued blessings. Continued work. Complete obedience. Worship Me in spirit and in truth. I've done a work in you.

Multiply, subdue, replenish, you have dominion. You are in the land of plenty. Lack and limitation, you don't have any. What you see right now isn't all I've done and shall continue to do for you. Keep riding in the chariot. You are in charge.

Love Me from the heart. I will never depart. You are set apart. You are the chosen one to get the work done. You believe in My son. In Christ Jesus is where you shall continue to be. The flesh has been crucified. You didn't just survive. You thrived.

I have provided, enjoy the ride. Keep riding high. The fire shall always be in front of you. This means Holy Ghost will always lead. Higher and higher you shall go. Stand behind the fire, never go before because you will burn or be destroyed.

*The Great Commission*

As long as the fire leads, everything that's in the way of your destiny can't stay. Never take your eye off the fire. Feed and focus on the flames, in Jesus' name.

You reign, you rule, everything opposite of God had been removed. Receive. Thanksgiving is a great key. Keep obeying Me. This place is where I want you to be. Enjoy, it's all from Me. I'm pleased.

**August 26, 2018**
Hello everyone. It's another great day to hear God. Another day of 6 a.m. prayer, He's called me to pray and intercede for the people.

**Tear Duct Functionality**
**Look at what He said this day:** The tear glands (lacrimal glands) located above each eyeball, continuously supply tear fluid that's wiped across the surface of your eye each time you blink your eyelids. Excess fluid drains through the tear ducts into the nose.

Just as this is important to our eyes, the Holy Spirit is also as important to our spirit and souls. Use this as an example of how Holy Spirit leads and feeds. We must allow him to lead the way by obeying what he says. Without Holy Spirit, we can lose our direction and never make it to our divine destinations.

**First thing, let's look at how important our tear ducts are:** If you can't use your eyes to see, then you won't know where you are going. If your vision is blocked, things could be in the way of your path and you can't see the right direction. Basically you could end up in the ditch of despair, going nowhere. You could be devastated, disrupted, and destroyed.

We must keep the tear ducts free and clear, from all things that appear, or anything that comes near. Protect it from all blockages, so that nothing stops it. If anything sneaks in without our knowledge, we must make the correction, and follow the directions of the doctor. First and foremost, we must recognize there's a problem.

**Connect** with the **Doctor.**

**Confess** and **Cancel** the **Disease.**

**Correct** the **Dysfunction.**

**Confidence** in the **Deliver.**

Which is God Himself. Trust and rely on Him, that it's already done, by grace through faith.

**See how important Holy Spirit is to us:** Without his leadership we are lost. We wouldn't know about Jesus on the cross. He paid the cost. The death, burial, and resurrection are our connection for directions. The power that we have received is all because of His lead. The fire is released after the Holy Ghost has come upon thee.

We have authority, strength, and might; as we've received our sight. We see where God wants us to be.

If there's danger, he instructs us to go the other way. God's protection is with us every day. He gives us wisdom, knowledge, and understanding of God's Word. He gives directions on how to obey God in every way. We must trust him wholeheartedly.

Never flee. Hear, listen, and do what he says to do. We can never be or go wrong when we allow him to come along. Take him everywhere, and he will always be there: He's never going anywhere. He's our heavenly help, and we don't have to worry about anything else.

Yes, we do trust man when he's operating in God's plans. Holy Spirit assists us to do everything in Christ Jesus. In Christ Jesus, we live, move, and have our total being. We receive the deeper things from God by **The Three: The Trinity — God the father, God the son, and God the Holy Spirit.**

**We command our angels to bring it all to us. This is a must.** Praise God! Awesome word today! Thank you Lord!

**August 27, 2018**

Good morning! This is the last day of 6 a.m. prayer on Facebook Live. When I started praying on there, God told me to pray, and He didn't say for how long. I just obeyed. Today, He woke me up earlier than usual and said, "It's your last day praying on there."

I said, "Wow! That was a short time. Eight days?" He answered my question by telling me He wanted to teach me discipline, and train me for my next assignment, which is getting GCW Ministry back going in full force. He told me I had to go to another level of my daily spiritual workout. Praise God! I receive.

God told me I would do things with GCW Ministry in an explosive way. He has allowed the people to know who Lady Mary Hatter is in an awesome way, and they will hear what I have to say.

Holy Spirit will continue to lead and feed me, so that the people will always receive what He's said and continues to say. They will obey God. To God be the glory!

People will begin to call me to teach. They will have me come to pray for the people. Even world organizations will ask me to come pray for people. Because I've commanded the angels to go and minister to the people who will bring me in to assist them in teaching, reaching, praying, and helping people get saved and come into the kingdom of God.

The Great Commission message and 5 Steps to Witnessing messages will be heard through me, by way of Holy Spirit. The prayer and being filled with Holy Spirit messages will also be heard across the world.

I will be teaching on giving, living righteously, believing, and expecting that by grace through faith all heavenly and earthly blessings have been released, and the manifestations will keep coming.

Since I've obeyed God, the books He's allowed me to write and continue to write will bring increase, abundance, and multiplication like never before. I shall receive from all opened doors. Doors that were shut and should have been open, are now opened.

No one can stop what He's started. The greater work has begun. I have victory because of His son. The gates are opened; enter in. Windows are opened, outpouring and overflowing on me now. Hallelujah! I receive now.

People will receive like never before. People begin and never stop coming through KMC's open doors. Healing, and deliverance, the captives have been set free. Money shall continue to come to me. Because of your obedience others are set free. Everything needed for the kingdom of God is released.

People will receive Jesus like never before. They will desire more and more. Because we've made God our source, we will always have resources. We will continue in faith, and money will keep coming our way.

# Conclusion

In all that we went through, God continued to be there, even though sometimes it looked as if He wasn't. We had to have faith like never before. Times were tough, however we kept trusting in Him and continue to trust in Him. Did we have doubt sometimes? Yes. We had to condition our minds at all times.

The blood of Jesus is key. I had to cast out all evil thoughts from me. Were there questions? Yes. In all that I shared, in the beginning I was scared. Hurricane Ike couldn't even be compared. We continued to rest in God's promises, as the Hurricane kept coming.

There were lessons learned. Because we were from Chicago we didn't properly prepare, and we weren't as concerned as we should've been because of the directions from the Mayor. He assured us that it wasn't going to be as devastating as people were saying.

We understand now, he didn't want people in a panic and rushing out of the area. This Hurricane definitely altered our lifestyle; we didn't know we would be in this situation for a while. Through it all, I retained my smile. God is awesome!

My husband, daughter, and grandchildren we are all still together. I'm grateful to God always. He continues to bless us every day. I'm always thankful to Him for just being God, and God alone.

Even through as of today we are still out of our home, resources continue to come. It's been a task getting them, with so much paperwork to complete to receive from Hurricane Harvey relief.

With our home not being in a flood zone, we were told we didn't need flood insurance. Lesson learned! In Texas, get it anyway. We have learned from this mistake. Many neighbors were without flood insurance.

We depended on the resources that God allowed us to receive. My husband's job was also a blessing. He continues to work, however we continued staying in faith as I reached out to the resources while believing money would keep coming our way. We have to do something while believing — money won't fall out of trees.

We understand that money isn't our source, God is. He has provided the resources. We have to keep putting our faith into action. Faith without works is dead.

Today marks the anniversary of Hurricane Harvey for us — this Hurricane that took all our stuff. Although it's been rough, we never lost our trust. Staying faithful is a must. Being filled with Holy Spirit is a plus. Trusting and relying on God with all our hearts, we will never depart.

Do things come and try to pull us apart? Yes. We understand that the enemy needs our help to destroy us. We have chosen not to help him out. As my husband, Pastor AD Hatter, says, "God can't function legally on this earth without a body." We have to do something to help God help us.

We must be in partnership with the trinity and His divinity — God the father, God the son, and God the Holy Ghost. We must command our angels to bring it all in, and we will continue to win, over and over again.

It's been my pleasure communicating with you. Thanks for joining in at the table, sitting, hearing, listening, and hopefully doing. It's my prayer that the lost will continue to be found. I will attach

*Conclusion*

at the very end, a prayer of salvation, and an invitation to be filled with Holy Spirit.

After reading this book, if you haven't receive salvation, I believe you will receive. I thank God almighty for using me. It's already done. You have won, because of God's son. Welcome to the family. I speak blessings always in your life. I Thank God for His son Jesus Christ. Enjoy your life! You only have one. Stay in God's Love; you never know when your spirit will be received above.

**Prayer to be Saved**

Dear God thank you for your word. I know without Jesus I am lost. I believe your word and if I ask you to save me and come into my heart you will. Jesus I give you the throne of my life, I turn my back on my old way of living and from this day forward I choose to please you with my life. I confess with thy mouth the Lord Jesus, and I believe in my heart that God hath raised him from the dead; Now fill me with your spirit and power so I can live a life pleasing in your sight. In Jesus name thank you father for saving me.

> That if thou shalt confess with thy mouth the Lord Jesus, and shalt believe in thine heart that God hath raised him from the dead, thou shalt be saved. For with the heart man believeth unto righteousness; and with the mouth confession is made unto salvation.
>
> For whosoever shall call upon the name of the Lord shall be saved."
>
> **Romans 10:9-10, 13 KJV**

**Prayer to Be Filled with Holy Spirit**

My heavenly Father, I am a believer. I am your child and you are my Father. Jesus is my Lord. I believe with all my heart that your Word is true. Your Word says that, if I will ask, I will receive the Holy Spirit, so in the name of Jesus Christ, my Lord, I am asking you to fill me to overflowing with your precious Holy Spirit. Baptize me in the Holy Spirit. Because of your Word, I believe that I now receive and I thank you for it. I believe that the Holy Spirit is within me and, by faith, I accept it. Now, Holy Spirit, rise up within me as I praise my God. I fully expect to speak with other tongues, as you give me the utterance.

**Meditate on these scriptures on Holy Spirit**: John 14:10,12,16-17; Acts 1:8; Acts 2:4, 32-33, 39; Acts 8:12-17; Acts 10:44-46; Acts 19:2, 5-6; 1 Corinthians 14:2-15, 18, 27; Ephesians 6:18; Jude 20

*If you enjoyed this book,*
*please check out Lady Mary's other books:*

### The Secrets Are Out: Nothing Happens Until the Secrets Are Revealed!
This powerful and awesome book will allow you to live and love life. Even though you might face troubled situations in life, God has allowed you to know what His Word says about it. You can come through everything that comes against you, when you obey what He says to do. God's secrets revealed are for you to rest, reign, rule, remain, and receive.

### Book of Revelations: Divine Disclosures of Best Kept Secrets!:
This is another awesome book of revealed secrets from God, which He has blessed me to write, and I know it will bless the body of Christ. Believers must believe these two key truths: 1) God is NOT a man. 2) God DOES NOT lie.

### T.S.I.T.S.: Things Seen in the Spirit:
God's Word Spoken in Faith, Believing, that He Will Bring it to Pass According to His Will for Our Lives: God is so awesome! He has allowed me to hear from Him like never before. As I pray daily and communicate with God and begin to listen to Him; He shares secrets with me to be revealed to the world. First God speaks what He wants to happen, how He wants it done and who He wants to do His work.

### Confessions Journal
Lady Mary Hatter's writing will inspire you, as she shares secrets from God through confessions spoken to her by His Spirit. Confessions from this book will help you to receive everything you want in the Kingdom and everything you want in every area of your life, your family and friend's lives.

**God's Decrees Spoken By Me, I Receive! Thank You Lord, for the Increase!**

This awesome book of Decrees will teach you what to speak and how to receive. This book allows you to speak His promotions, promises, provisions, peace and prosperity. This book also speaks revelations, restoration, redemption, and helps reassign and realign things in your life.

In this book you will learn how to live and love life by speaking out your mouths what God says, and do what He says do, so that all His blessings shall keep coming to you. We decree manifestations, because we are a blessed generation and generations to come. It is God's will being done. Decrees are for our victory, and for all the world to see. We have His-story! We are made in His image. So is Jesus, so are we: because of His Decrees, we can and will live in prosperity! Receive all these Decrees!

# Invite Christian Teacher
# Lady Mary Hatter
## to speak at your church or event

Lady Mary helps people walk in their purpose; which is to build up the Kingdom of God first, and then they can live effective, efficient, and excellent lives, in order to experience all that God has already promised them.

Life Coaching and Author Coaching services are also available.

Follow her on social media:

**Facebook:** Upe Deisgns Tsits
**Twitter:** @LadyMaryHatter
**Amazon:** Click her author page and follow her

To book Lady Mary, please call
**281.254.5994**
or visit her website and fill out the contact form.

## www.MaryHatter.com